INSIGHT

Pe...
& Langkawi

Discovery
CHANNEL

APA PUBLICATIONS
Part of the Langenscheidt Publishing Group

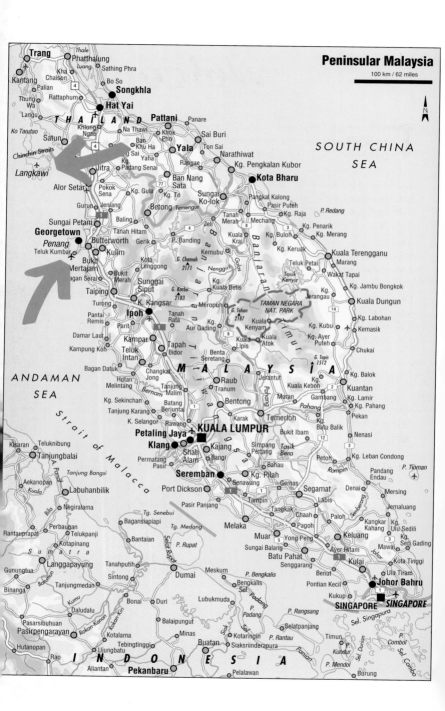

Peninsular Malaysia

100 km / 62 miles

N

Welcome

This is one of 133 itinerary-based Pocket Guides produced by the editors of Insight Guides, whose books have set the standard for visual travel guides since 1970. With top-quality photography and authoritative recommendations, this guidebook brings you the very best of Penang and Langkawi in a series of tailor-made itineraries devised by Insight's Malaysia-based correspondent, SL Wong.

Penang and Langkawi are two of Malaysia's best-known island destinations. While they share a common history and are located in the Straits of Malacca, each has a vastly different appeal to tourists. The former is steeped in history and culture, the latter charms with its natural beauty. This book outlines seven itineraries for Penang and another seven for Langkawi. For each destination, the first few itineraries cover the most essential sights and reveal the charms of the place. The remaining itineraries introduce you to specific aspects of the islands or go off the beaten track.

Chapters on shopping, eating out and nightlife, plus a practical information section covering travel essentials, complete this reader-friendly guide.

SL Wong is a Malaysia-born freelance writer who specialises in travel, environment and technology. She has worked and lived in Australia, Singapore and Hong Kong, and travelled the length and breadth of Malaysia. She knows Penang intimately as her maternal hometown, adores its food and the old-world charm, and is proud that it is part of her Straits Chinese heritage. She has also seen Langkawi evolve into a top tourist destination over the years, and is glad that it continues to enchant with its rustic lifestyle, the palm-lined beaches and amazing rainforests. Wong is also the author of *Insight Pocket Guide Kuala Lumpur*.

Pages 2/3: trishaw in front of the Town Hall in Georgetown
Pages 8/9: sunset at Bon Ton resort in Langkawi

History & Culture

history/culture

With its strategic location on the Straits of Malacca and aided by southwesterly and northeasterly monsoons, the Malay peninsula has for centuries enjoyed mutually beneficial trade relationships with India, the Middle East, Europe and China. The interaction also saw a cross-pollination of knowledge, belief systems, culture and language that over long periods of time fed into existing indigenous systems.

Trade Routes: Crossing Cultures

Penang and Langkawi were part of one of the most important early centres of trade in the northern peninsula: Kedah. Specifically, Kedah, known in ancient texts as Kadaram or Kataha, was an important centre of early Indian influence and commerce. In fact, Kedah appears in Malay folklore as part of one of the Malay world's early settlements, Langkasuka (Lang-Ya-Hsin to Chinese travellers). This Indian kingdom was said to have been founded by a Prince Marong Mahawangsa in the second century in Patani, south Thailand, and the name 'Langkawi' is a likely reference to that ancient monarchy.

Muslims

Indians probably came to the Malay archipelago in search of spices, sandalwood and gold, possibly even before the 1st century. They brought with them Buddhism and Hinduism, as well as rituals, vocabulary, stories and notions of kingship still preserved in Malay courts today. The Malay world also formed links with a Muslim trading network that used Arab and Persian trade routes in their business transactions with China. By the 9th century, Kedah (Kalah to the Muslim traders) was firmly marked on maps as a transit point. By the 13th century, Muslim trading based particularly in the west coast of India had become more prominent. In the Malay world, Indian Muslims played a critical role in spreading Islam locally.

The Chinese

The trading relationship between Kedah and China began when China embarked on maritime trade in the 5th century. Chinese public relations with Southeast Asia were particularly strengthened in the 15th century through voyages by the Chinese explorer Admiral Cheng Ho. For the Malay world, trade with China saw the exchange of material goods and the introduction of materials, technologies and skills.

Left: Penang ferry crossing at sunset
Right: assortment of spices

One reason why ports such as Langkasuka flourished was favourable winds – ships that sailed to the Malay Peninsula with one monsoon had to remain there until the winds changed. These centres of trade became influential maritime powers, which eventually came under the power of the great empire Srivijaya in the 7th century, Majapahit in the 13th century, and finally Malacca two centuries later. It was the embracing of Islam by Malacca that attracted wealthy Muslim traders and contributed to its meteoric rise as a commercial centre. Islam also spread to the region through this empire.

Colonialists and Economic Progress

However, markets in the tradition of Malacca never emerged again after the state fell to the Portuguese in the 16th century and the Dutch in the 17th century. These colonialists had trading policies that constrained international commerce, and like the British who came after them, they set up centres that they controlled and maintained only for their own benefit.

In the 18th century, a time of economic opportunities, Muslim Indian traders thrived. Another influential group was the Arabs, particularly those from the Hadramaut. Respected for being of the same race as the Prophet, the Arabs had special commercial privileges and traded extensively in the archipelago. Migrant Chinese numbers also swelled, and many went into the lucrative agricultural and mining sectors. Groups aligned themselves with different Malay rulers and, as the economy improved, conflicts over territorial rights and succession grew. Meanwhile, the English, through the East India Company, controlled the cloth-producing and poppy-growing areas in India, and made advances in the maritime industry.

Kedah and the northern Malay states had long been vassal states to Siam. Hoping to gain protection from these overlords, the Sultan of Kedah leased Penang to the East India Company in 1786 and signed a treaty with them in 1791. In 1800, Province Wellesly (Seberang Prai) was ceded to the British.

Above: the British East India Company headquarters in Penang, c. 1850

history/culture

However, the British did not keep their end of the bargain (to offer military protection), but Penang still became a British free trade port, and, as part of the Straits Settlements (with Singapore and Malacca), it was the entry point for eventual British colonial rule throughout the Malay peninsula.

By the 19th century, British presence in the Malay peninsula had eroded local multiracial power bases. The British also created separate administrative categories and interests based on ethnicity. In addition, that period saw the establishing of political boundaries and administration which became the basis of the Malaysia that gained independence in 1957. Today, almost half a century later, racialised politics remain a challenge to Malaysians but they have found the means to thrive in their cultural diversity.

PENANG

The earliest record of Penang's name was Ping-Lang-Seu, in a 1621 chart based on Admiral Cheng Ho's voyages. It is thought that this name had been in use since the 15th century. However, local names in other languages might have preceded this. They include Pulau, Pulo and Pooloo or Penang, Pinang, Pinam and Pinaon. 'Pinang' is Malay for betelnut, an important product in Malay culture, as it is used in everything from weddings to makeup, and as a popular chewable snack.

Penang's exposure to other cultures goes back to the 14th century, when Portuguese traders from India stopped there to replenish water and food and to trade with the villagers. The place where they stopped most often was Batu Ferringhi (Ferringhi's Rock).

The British officer behind the ceding of Penang in 1786 by Kedah to the East India Company was Francis Light, a midshipman who was good friends with the Sultan of Kedah. He became the free port's first superintendent and built the capital, naming it after George IV.

Georgetown

There is an interesting tale of how the enterprising Light laid the foundations for Georgetown. The site he had chosen, where Fort Cornwallis is, was a forest with such dense wood that tools proved too weak and the labour mutinied. Light came up with the ingenious idea of filling a cannon with silver dollars and firing it into the jungle. The incentive worked and from here, a neat grid of houses was soon established. The original streets, Light Street, Beach Street, Malabar Street (now renamed as Chulia Street) and Pitt Street (now renamed as Jalan Masjid Kapitan Kling) still stand today.

The Straits Chinese

European and Asian settlements were demarcated and settlers from all over came to call the city home. Sizable Penang communities include the Straits Chinese. The core of the Straits Chinese, also known as Baba or Nonya, or Peranakan (local born) Chinese, are early migrants from China who adopted Malay customs and/or married Malays,

Right: cultural diversity is etched in Penang's faces

but retained their Chinese culture. They lived mainly in the Straits Settlement states of Penang, Malacca and Singapore and spoke local Malay dialects as well as Hokkien, which is infused with Malay and Thai words. The Penang Straits Chinese were also more anglicised than the Chinese from China, who came later. Other aspects of Straits Chinese culture are manifest in their dress, food as well as architecture.

Indian Muslims

The Indian Muslims – once known as the Jawi-Peranakan, and now commonly referred to as Mamak – are the descendants of the powerful traders from India who settled down in the peninsula. The largest group is Tamil, but there are also Bengali, Malabari and Gujerati. They were astute at running businesses, particularly in shipping and imports.

The Indian Muslims played a major role in the spreading of Islam. They built the first mosque on the island, Masjid Kapitan Kling. They also paid great attention to social services, published the country's first Jawi newspaper, and formed one of the first political parties in the country.

The spread of Islam was also propagated by the Arabs and Achehnese. Invited to Penang by Light to participate in the spice trade, they established settlements on the island. The majority of the Arab community were from the Hadramaut, and today almost every Muslim in Penang is related by marriage to Penang Arabs. Politically, Arabs today have been assimilated into the ethnic grouping of 'Malay', but they retain aspects of their own culture.

Eurasians

Penang's Eurasians are descendants of mainly Portuguese settlers who married Siamese and Burmese women. They were originally from Phuket, but moved to Kedah to escape political persecution. Light himself arranged for the first Roman Catholic community to be brought over from the mainland, and employed Eurasian Catholics. There was a personal dimension to his decision: Light's wife was Eurasian.

New Technologies

Numerous other communities called Penang home and, at the turn of the 20th century, trade – involving mainly pepper, tin and rubber – continued to drive Penang's economy. The state's free port status was lifted in 1969, but manufacturing then became its economic mainstay with the establishment of the Silicon Valley-type electrical and electronics-manufacturing zone in Bayan Lepas. Aimed at the

Above: old postcard photograph of Victoria Pier
Right: the Bayan Lepas Free Industrial Zone

export market, manufacturing is the largest contributor to the economy and it boosted Penang's economy to third largest in the country.

In the new millennium, Penang is reinventing itself to counter the global slowdown in the demand for electronics and the threat of cheaper labour in China. In 2005, the city was granted cybercity status, paving the way for the development of information and communications technology industries which is part of a national move towards a knowledge- and service-based economy.

Architectural Heritage

Penang's biggest challenge today is the conservation of its historical and cultural wealth. Georgetown is awaiting listing as a World Heritage City; a status crucial to the conservation of a city still richly clothed in 19th and 20th century ethnic and British colonial influences. The rabid redevelopment that has overtaken many other cities in Malaysia, such as the country's capital, Kuala Lumpur, had been held at bay by a 1948 Rent Control Act.

However, when that Act was repealed at the turn of the 21st century, economics dictated that buildings be torn down, and mainstream development has seen the erection of hopelessly out-of-sync replacement towers of glass and metal. Rents have skyrocketed, and this has forced out many of the old tenants, and drained the vibrant inner city life of Georgetown. Thankfully, however, conservationists led by the dedicated Penang Heritage Trust and the Consumers' Association of Penang are backed by the government in their work to prevent the city's historic and cultural environment from being destroyed.

LANGKAWI

In contrast, Langkawi's man-made history is very new. Like Penang, it was for centuries a port of call for fresh water, but mainly for fishing vessels, and its many islands and bays provided shelter from storms for pirates. Unlike Penang, however, Langkawi did not feature in any grand political scheme for the Sultan of Kedah, nor did opportunistic Englishmen set up base here. As such, it was largely agrarian and untouched until former Prime Minister Tun Dr Mahathir Mohamad decided to transform it into a premier tourist destination.

Tourism Mecca

A son of Kedah, Mahathir personally took on this challenge of putting Langkawi on the tourist map. In 1990, a federal body under the Ministry of Finance was charged with developing the island, primarily by putting in place much-needed infrastructure. The decade following that saw intense building of roads, hotels, marinas and other tourist facilities, including a com-

Right: ex-Prime Minister Tun Dr Mahathir Mohamad at a signing ceremony

plete rebuilding of the main town of Kuah. The island was granted duty-free status and the makeup of the local population changed as other Malaysians and non-Malaysians moved here.

Today, Langkawi is often the focus of international events, such as the Langkawi International Maritime and Aerospace Exhibition, and international races such as the Le Tour de Langkawi. It is home to four marinas and close to established sailing destinations as Phuket; as such, plans have long been afoot to turn Langkawi into an international yacht registration centre.

Over the years, some tourist development efforts have worked better than others, but tourist numbers have swelled tenfold from 1987 to over 2 million arrivals in 2004. The dust from that intensive building is settling down, and the island is slowly developing its own image as a place of natural beauty and mystical charm, with a laid-back feeling. The good news is that development has remained within designated zones, and close attention has been paid to a maximum-four-storey-high ruling for buildings outside Kuah. Whatever forests remaining are protected as forest reserves, and there is a movement to gazette geological parks.

Myths and Legends

Legends and myths abound in Langkawi, colouring virtually every mountain, stream and settlement. A seminal legend is that of Mahsuri, a lass of great beauty who was wrongly accused of adultery. At her execution by *keris* (dagger), white blood spurted from her body, proving her innocence. With her last breath, she cursed the island to seven generations of bad luck. Whether or not Mahsuri did actually live, the people believe that the bad spell came to an end in the mid-1980s, which coincidentally was around the time Langkawi was granted duty-free status.

Local Culture

Culturally, Langkawi is Malay, with its original population living in villages that have been modernised with the new tourist money, but remain essentially communal in lifestyle. Sharing and cooperation are emphasised, and religion – Islam – is a key part of life. While some locals have started small businesses, many have continued with traditional lifestyles, including farming and fishing. Meanwhile, the northern part of Langkawi is very Thai, and a mixture of Thai and Malay is spoken here. There is also a large and established community of Thai and Burmese fishing folk.

Above: crystal-clear waters at Langkawi's Pulau Payar Marine Park

HISTORY HIGHLIGHTS

1st century Langkasuka is established.

4th–7th century The Hindu-Buddhist kingdom, Bujang Valley, is established.

7th–8th century Kedah under the influence of the Sumatran kingdom of Srivijaya. Kedah dominated by Siam.

14th century Portuguese traders from India to China stop in Penang to replenish water supplies.

1786 The Sultan of Kedah cedes Penang to the British East India Company. Penang is established as the first British trading post in the Far East.

1816 Penang Free School, the first school in Malaysia, is founded.

1821 Kedah directly under Thai rule.

1824 The Anglo-Dutch Treaty partitions the Malay world through the Straits of Malacca. The peninsula comes under the British and Indonesia to the Dutch.

1826 The formation of the Straits Settlements, comprising Penang, Singapore and Malacca, allows British influence to extend throughout the peninsula.

1840s Tin is discovered in Perak and Penang becomes a key collection and export centre.

1867 The British Colonial Office takes direct control of Penang, and it officially becomes a crown colony.

1874 The Pangkor Treaty sees the setting up of the British Resident system, significantly increasing British political control in the peninsula.

1896 Formation of the Federated Malay States as a British Protectorate, with Kuala Lumpur as its capital.

1905 The first hydroelectric scheme in Penang is completed, and this gives the island electricity.

1909 The Anglo-Siamese Treaty transfers Kedah from Siamese power to British rule.

1910 The rising demand for rubber from the West turns Penang once again into a major port.

1941 In WWII, Japan invades Peninsular Malaysia, and Penang is bombed; the British flee.

1945 Japan formally surrenders and World War II ends.

1957 Malaya gains independence from the British and Penang and Kedah becomes two of the states of the newly formed Federation of Malaya. Tunku Abdul Rahman is Malaysia's first Prime Minister. In addition, Georgetown is awarded city status.

1963 Malaysia is formed.

1969 Penang loses its free port status.

1970 Tun Abdul Razak becomes Malaysia's second Prime Minister.

1970s Penang becomes the site of Malaysia's first free trade zone. The Bayan Lepas Free Industrial Zone has become one of Asia's largest electrical and electronics manufacturing centres.

1981 Tun Dr Mahathir Mohamad becomes Malaysia's third Prime Minister. He would become one of Asia's longest serving heads of state.

1985 Penang Bridge is built to join Penang island to the mainland.

1987 In January, Langkawi is declared a duty-free port.

1989 Langkawi hosts the 1989 Commonwealth Heads of Government Meeting (CHOGM).

1990 Langkawi Development Authority is established to oversee the development of Langkawi into a major regional tourist destination.

1991 The New Development Policy (Vision 2020) takes effect, its aim being to make Malaysia a developed nation by 2020.

1996 Malaysia's first satellite, MEASAT I is launched. Langkawi is the site of the Satellite Control Centre.

1997 The Asian financial crisis hits Malaysia. Financial controls are put in place.

2001 Langkawi is declared a tourism city. Malaysia's economy rebounds.

2003 Datuk Seri Abdullah Ahmad Badawi becomes Malaysia's fourth Prime Minister.

2005 Penang is awarded cybercity status. Capital controls are lifted.

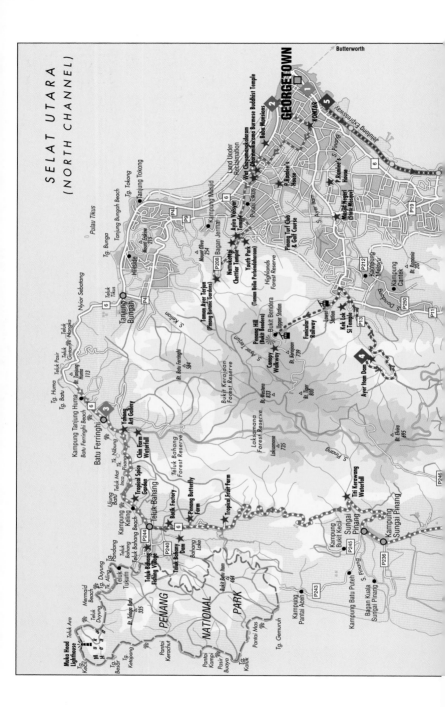

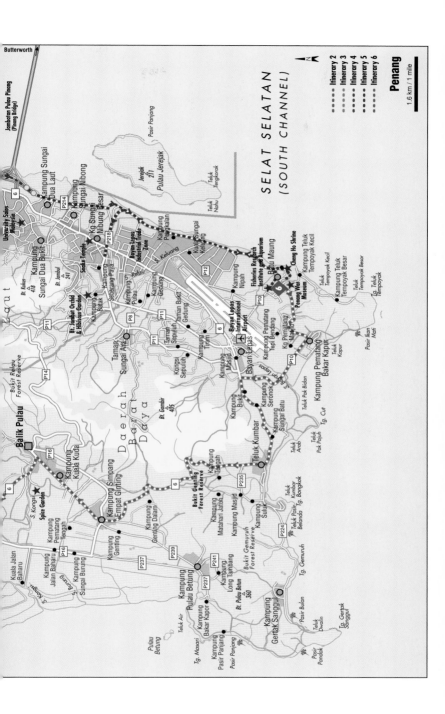

Penang

1.6 km / 1 mile

••••• Itinerary 2
••••• Itinerary 3
••••• Itinerary 4
••••• Itinerary 5
••••• Itinerary 6

Penang
Itineraries

Shaped like a pregnant turtle, Penang island is one of the oldest and most popular tourist destinations in Malaysia. Officially known as Pulau Pinang, it is located in the northeast of Peninsular Malaysia and comprises not only an island but also a strip of land on the mainland known as Seberang Prai or Butterworth. However, it is the 285-sq-km (110-sq-mile) island that is the tourist magnet, known once upon a time for its beaches, and now for its cultural and historical heritage.

Penang's beautiful capital, Georgetown, is in the northwestern part of the island, and still arranged according to the grid on which it was first built in the late 18th century. Urban development and agriculture have spread to most of the plains around the central highlands. The famous beaches, which are still good for a relaxing seaside get-away, are located to the north of Georgetown and the industrial area is in the southwest, where the airport is situated. The western side is relatively agrarian.

The first itinerary and part of the second one shows off some of Georgetown's important historical sites. To fully appreciate the story behind Georgetown, it is worthwhile joining a heritage tour or hiring a knowledgeable guide. Alternatively, the curious traveller with plenty of time will enjoy wandering the streets, delighting in new discoveries. Georgetown has much to offer early risers and late-night revellers. This makes it an attractive place to base yourself; what's more, it has a range of accommodation to suit any budget.

For a beach resort holiday, however, it is best to opt for a place at one of the beaches. While development has meant that these beaches have lost some of their lustre, the famous Batu Ferringhi is still attractive, and you will discover this in Itinerary 3.

The next four itineraries will show you the way to the hills and to Penang's less populated parts. Included are hikes, driving tours and journeys to the past.

To get around Georgetown, avoid driving as traffic is horrific and the one-way streets are difficult to navigate by car. Also, while buses do go to every part of the island, they are slow and unreliable. Your best bet would be to hire a taxi, or a car with a driver, and to time your trips to avoid rush hour. Driving outside of Georgetown is, however, quite nice.

It is worth noting that the locals, particularly the older generation, refer to the roads by their colonial rather than Malay names, so it is 'Penang Street' rather than 'Lebuh Penang', and 'Pitt Street' instead of 'Jalan Masjid Kapitan Kling'.

Left: the upward sweep of the Kwan Yin Teng roof
Right: a street vendor plying his ware

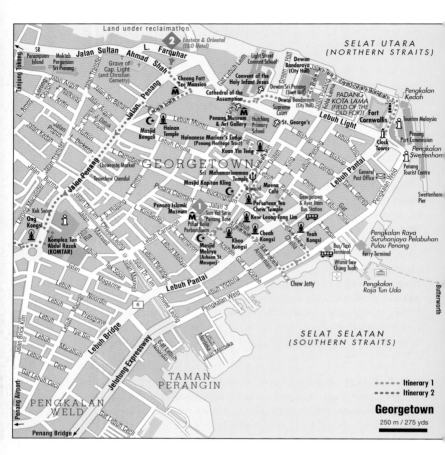

Georgetown
250 m / 275 yds

····· Itinerary 1
····· Itinerary 2

1. GEORGETOWN HERITAGE TRAIL *(see map, above)*

This essential tour of the capital is a day-long walkabout covering the key historical sites. Soak in the capital's fascinating and complex ethnic influences and colonial British heritage.

This walk is most similar to the first of two Heritage Trails designed by the Penang Heritage Trust, but follows a different route. The Heritage Trail maps are worth getting for their detailed information on the sights you encounter along the way. Get your copy from the Trust (Mon–Fri 9am–5pm, Sat 9am–1pm; tel: 04-264 2631); you can also sign up for a guided tour here. This itinerary can also be done by trishaw. Just hail one down by the road or head to the trishaw station close to the start of this trail, outside the Cititel Hotel on Jalan Penang. Yet another option is to use the free hop-on hop-off bus shuttle service that takes 45 minutes to go around town – get a map from your hotel or download it from www.tourismpenang.gov.my.

Start in **Lebuh Armenian**. In the late 19th century, this was a bustling centre for Malay and Sumatran traders, as well as for Muslim pilgrims on the

Top right: an open Koran is displayed at the Penang Islamic Museum
Bottom right: the impressive facade of the Khoo Kongsi

haj. The spread of Islam in Penang and the establishment of mosques are closely associated with the Arabs. The history of this area and of Penang Muslims can be reviewed in the **Penang Islamic Museum** (daily 9.30am–6pm, closed Tue; admission charge; www.penangislamicmuseum.net), situated on the corner of Lebuh Armenian and Lebuh Acheh. The museum occupies a restored mansion once owned by Syed Mohamad Alatas, a wealthy Arab merchant. Alatas was a community leader who traded with the Achehnese and supported

them when they were besieged by the Dutch in the 1870s. The museum space makes for a nice wander and its photographs are noteworthy.

The Arab/Achenese enclave in Lebuh Aceh was actually established by another rich merchant, Tengku Syed Hussain Al-Aidid, who built **Masjid Melayu** (daily; free) or Acheen Street Mosque, another important Arabic monument. To get to there from the museum, turn left into Lebuh Acheh and walk for about 50m (160ft). Small and unassuming, the mosque nonetheless incorporates Achehnese, Anglo-Indian and Chinese elements. Today, it retains its original 1808 design except for two additions – Moorish arches and a small single window in the minaret believed to have been a hole caused by a cannonball fired during the 1867 triad riots.

The Chinese Influence

Economic opportunities in the Malay world were what attracted Chinese escaping from extreme poverty in China. Among others, they brought with them business and social models such as the *kongsi* – associations of individuals from the same dialect group and from the same part of China. These

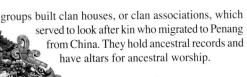

groups built clan houses, or clan associations, which served to look after kin who migrated to Penang from China. They hold ancestral records and have altars for ancestral worship.

Khoo Kongsi

The most magnificent of the clan houses is the **Khoo Kongsi** (daily 9am–5pm; admission charge; www.khookongsi.com.my), with its elaborate stone reliefs, woodcarvings and porcelain shardwork. Its entrance is opposite the mosque along Lebuh Cannon. This clan house is owned by one of the richest Chinese clans in the northern region – the Khoos.

Soon after the Khoo Kongsi was built in 1901, it burned down mysteriously. Some say its opulence angered the gods; others believed it was the Chinese emperor who was upset. A more modest but still well ornamented replacement was erected, and more recently it benefitted from a million-ringgit award-winning restoration. A useful aid as you explore this edifice is the commemorative booklet that you can buy at the teahouse-cum-souvenir shop in the basement. The simpler but no less interesting clanhouses of the Cheah and Yap families are nearby, and they are also worth a visit.

Chinese Water Villages

Clans also lived together, and the six clan jetties in **Pengkalan Weld** are a living historical testament to this. From the Khoo Kongsi, walk out through the Lebuh Armenian exit and down the road into Gat Lebuh Armenian until you reach the Pengkalan Weld junction. Across the road is a conglomeration of wooden stilt houses linked by plank walkways spread over kilometres of murky waterfront. Each clan jetty is fronted by a Chinese temple.

Immediately facing the Pengkalan Weld junction is the largest jetty, the **Chew Jetty**. Opposite its clan temple is a stage for traditional Chinese opera, which is performed during Chinese festivals. Walk down the 1-km (½-mile)-long walkway to the end. Be polite as you go through, as these are homes; in the case of the Chews, by fishermen and petty traders.

Little India

This should bring you to lunchtime. Head to **Little India** for a spicy banana leaf meal; it is a 10-minute walk. From the Chew Jetty, turn right, back into Pengkalan Weld, then cross into Gat Lebuh Chulia. When you hit Lebuh Penang, turn right to get to **Meena Café** (daily 7.30am–10pm; tel: 04-261 4349) and try its famous ice-cold mango *lassi* (yoghurt drink) and *briyani* rice set.

Little India is where Indian merchants or Chulias settled. Said to have come to Penang with the British, they were Hindu, and it is this Penang Hindu diaspora that is believed to have played a role in significantly perpetuating the Hindu cultural heritage in the country. Certainly the Chulias built the most temples.

The first Hindu temple, the **Sri Mahamariamman Temple** (daily; free), is named after the goddess of health and rain, and was built by the Nattukottai Chettiars, a diasporic community from south India whose members were the fathers of modern banking. The Chettiars built temples everywhere they settled so they could worship Lord Shiva and his son, Lord Muruga.

To find your way to this temple from the restaurant, head out again to Lebuh Chulia, turn right, and then right again two streets later into Lebuh Queen. Remove your shoes and go through the *goparam,* or sculptured entrance gate, which features sculptures of gods and goddesses, the work of master craftsmen from India. Inside the temple is a bejewelled statue of Lord Muruga.

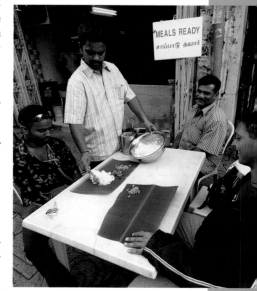

The Chettiars

The Chettiars are known for their business acumen, and they pioneered banking in the region. In pre-war Penang, as in many parts of Malaysia, they were almost solely responsible for driving the economy. So synonymous did they become with moneylending, the word *chettiar* has been absorbed into local parlance to mean 'money-lender'. However, in the face of modern banking and the takeover of the industry by loan sharks, modern Chettiars have distanced themselves from the traditional business and turned to other professions. However, their religious legacy remains in the shape of *chettiar* temples (*see also Itinerary 2*) and the colourful Thaipusam festival celebrating Muruga.

Top left: Khoo Kongsi roof detail; **Bottom left:** Chinese opera performer getting ready; **Right:** a banana leaf curry meal being served in Little India

Actually, the first Indians to arrive in Penang were Muslim. Like the Arabs, they thrived on the spice trade with Acheh and Europe. They built the first mosque in Penang, the **Masjid Kapitan Kling** (daily; free), naming it after their Kapitan Kling or Indian-Muslim merchant headman, Caudeer Mohudeen. From the Sri Mahamariamman Temple, turn right into Lebuh Chulia and walk to Jalan Masjid Kapitan Kling. Turn left to get to the mosque entrance.

The mosque's domes and arches, first redesigned in 1916 by British architects and given a second facelift in the 1930s, are in the Moghul Revival fashion. The original structure was, by contrast, very simple.

Goddess of Mercy Temple

After exploring the mosque, turn left into Jalan Masjid Kapitan Kling again and head towards **Kuan Yin Teng** (daily; free), about 100m (300ft) away. The two-century-old temple is named after Kuan Yin or the Goddess of Mercy, one of the most popular deities worshipped by Taoists. It is one of the busiest temples in Georgetown, particularly on auspicious full moon days, Wesak days and the three enlightenment days of Kuan Yin. Another deity is also worshipped here: **Ma Chor Poh**, the patron saint of seafarers, also known to Taoists as Mother of the Hearth. Look out also for little altars of other deities around the temple, especially around the venerated giant fig tree.

The Colonial Quarter

From Kuan Yin Teng, backtrack along Jalan Masjid Kapitan Kling and turn right into Lorong Stewart. You will come to the **Penang Heritage Trust** (www.pht.org.my; *see also page 22*) at 26A, which has excellent archives.

At the end of the road, turn right into **Love Lane**, a backpacker area full of cafes where you might want to cool down with a drink. Where Love Lane meets Lebuh Farquhar, take a right at the Cathedral of the Assumption and spend some time at the **Penang Museum and Art Gallery** (daily 9am–6pm, closed Wed; admission charge). Built as a school, it now houses exhibits of local communities, historic places and artwork. Of note are the Straits Chinese artefacts and oil paintings of Penang's landscapes in 1814–15 by Captain Robert Smith. Outside is a bronze statue of Francis Light, the man who negotiated the ceding of Penang to the East India Company. The statue is actually based on his son, Colonel William Light, who later founded Adelaide in Australia.

Walk out now to Lebuh Light,

Left: the Penang Heritage Trust office is worth a visit for its excellent materials

penang itineraries

past the **Light Street Convent School**, which served as accommodation for Francis Light and East India Company officials, and internment quarters for Japanese prisoners-of-war. When you see two elegant neo-classical buildings, cross the road. The **Dewan Sri Pinang** (Town Hall) and **Dewan Bandaraya** (City Hall) were built in the early 20th century, and feature graceful columns and balconies from which the elite would watch processions on the green. Today, as then, the **Padang Kota Lama** (Field of the Old Fort) is the venue for national day events and carnivals.

Fort Cornwallis

Walk towards the sea, and turn right into the **Esplanade** (Jalan Tun Syed Sheh Barkbah), popular among locals. At the end of the paved walkway is the entrance to **Fort Cornwallis** (daily 8.30am–6.30pm; admission charge). This is where Georgetown was first built. It was named after the Governor-General of the East India Company and built with convict labour. Today its ramparts enclose a history gallery; tour guides wear British colonial redcoats.

The ramparts are still guarded by old cannons, the most famous being the Seri Rambai. Originally presented by the Dutch to the Sultan of Johor in 1606, it was captured by Achenese forces, used as a gift in an alliance in the state of Selangor and finally brought to Penang by the Madras Native Infantry. Like many ancient weapons, it is considered sacred.

From here, walk along until you hit the **Clock Tower**, built by a rich Chinese businessman to commemorate the Diamond Jubilee of Queen Victoria. Quirky features are found in this four-tiered structure, such as a Moorish dome and arches, balconies and battlemented parapets. Finally, take a taxi back to Little India for a dinner of *tandoori* chicken and *naan* bread at **Kapitan's** (93 Lebuh Chulia; open 24 hours; tel: 04-264 1191).

Above: the famed Seri Rambai cannon
Right: the Clock Tower has unusual features

2. Penang Road, Temples and Gardens
(see map, p18–19 and p22)

This day-long tour covers Penang's landmarks, takes in some shopping and temples, and ends with an evening at the lush Botanic Gardens.

The morning section can be covered on foot or by trishaw. Book a taxi for the afternoon portion. Nature lovers might want to allocate more time for the Botanic Gardens, which has some short but lovely trails – maps can be purchased at the Gardens' bookshop.

Breakfast at the E&O

A combination of opulence and its owner's generosity brought worldwide fame to the **E&O Hotel** in the 1880s. Admirably, the hotel continues to live up to that fame today. Despite extensive renovations, it has maintained

its exotic Moorish architecture and 'an endless seafront', as well as an old-world atmosphere that conjures up its exclusive colonial patronage such as Somerset Maugham and Herman Hesse.

Capture some of that previous century feel by having breakfast at the **Verandah** (daily 6.30am–11pm; tel: 03-263 0630). Pick a table on the famous landscaped promenade by the sea, then take your pick from their extensive buffet spread, which includes freshly baked pastries and breads, eggs, yoghurt and coffee. Alternatively, go local with rice congee or *nasi lemak*.

Cheong Fatt Tze Mansion

Finish breakfast by 10.30am so that you have enough time for the day's tour. The next destination is the Cheong Fatt Tze Mansion. From the hotel, cross the road and walk straight towards Lebuh Light. Cross this road, turn left and continue to Lebuh Leith, where you turn right to see a blue building on your right. The **Cheong Fatt Tze Mansion** (daily tours 11am and 3pm; tel: 04-262 0006; www.cheongfatt tzemansion.com) is a marvel of Chinese *feng shui* (geomantic) architectural elements. Owned by China's last Mandarin, the mansion also houses hybrid Western and Eastern paraphernalia, including a rare porcelain collection, sculptures, tapestries and antiques. Take the excellent guided tour at 11am, which lasts an hour. Otherwise, the only other way you may explore this award-winning restoration project is by staying in one of its 16 designer rooms. Opposite the mansion is a row of buildings that were once the kitchen and servants' quarters, now a lively nook for dining and pubbing.

Continue down Leith Street and you will hit Jalan Penang or **Penang Road**. Offering everything from antiques and curios to leather goods and

Above: taking a dip at the E&O Hotel is a nostalgic affair
Top right: trishaws against the striking facade of the Cheong Fatt Tze Mansion

batik souvenirs, this main street and the streets off it are full of a local colour that an exploratory spirit and serendipity best reveal. It is about 20 minutes' walk to the famous KOMTAR tower at the end of Penang Road. Keep on the left side of the road, and, five minutes on, you will pass a gateway to **Campbell Street Mall**, once a prime shopping area, but now rather sanitised.

Chowrasta Market and Local Delicacies

Keep walking until the smell of wok-roasted chestnuts signals the **Chowrasta Market** in a multi-storey building on your left. This is a traditional morning **wet market**, where fresh produce and dry goods are sold. In the stalls outside the market, you can sample Penang's famous preserved and dried nutmeg and mango as well as an assortment of local biscuits.

Proceed down Penang Road, and you will see people clustered around a small stall in Lebuh Keng Swee, which is the small lane on your left. This is the famous **Teochew Chendul** stall, which hawks *cendol*, a popular dessert of flour paste and coconut milk. Do not be put off by the green colouring – it is merely *pandan* extract, a fragrant herb.

Next, you will come to a complex pedestrian flyover. Take the right passage, which takes you back to Penang Road (the right side). Along this stretch, you will pass souvenir shops and a Chinese coffeeshop that opened in 1906 – **Kek Seng**, famous for its ice cream, *ais kacang*

Right: *popiah* (spring roll) skin being hand-made by a vendor at Chowrasta Market

(shaved ice dessert), *koay teow th'ng* (flat noodle soup) and *lobak* (pork spring rolls).

Continue walking along Penang Road and you will come to a corner shop selling bright pink buns – this is *meeku* or traditional Chinese buns, used as offerings in Taoist worship at home or in temples, and during Chinese rites of marriage.

View from KOMTAR

Use the pedestrian crossing to get to Penang's tallest structure, **KOMTAR** (Kompleks Tun Abdul Razak), where you can get a bird's eye view of Georgetown from the 60th floor (daily 10am–10pm; admission charge; tel: 04-262 2222). Turn left from the pedestrian crossing, walk around the building past the post office and you will come to KOMTAR's front entrance. Note that the tower is sometimes closed for private functions.

It should now be about lunchtime. Take a taxi or a trishaw to Pulau Tikus. Get off near the market at the **Bee Hooi Coffeeshop** at the junction of Jalan Burma and Lorong Pulau Tikus. Here, there is excellent curry *mee* (noodles) available from 7–11am, and plenty of other hawker fare choices.

Buddhist Temples

After lunch, walk to Lorong Burma where two Buddhist temples sit facing each other. These are really community temples erected on land that was

endowed to Theravada Buddhists in 1845. Mostly Thai and Burmese, they have now been assimilated into Penang society, although they still occupy the houses in this area.

The **Wat Chayamangkalaram** (daily 6am–5.30pm; free) features typical Thai elements in its architecture and in the presence of mythical creatures, such as the *nak* or serpent gods, which are in the traditional position of guarding the temple entrance. Inside the main temple is an impressive gold-plated reclining Buddha. The temple walls are also covered with thousands of Buddhas. Note that photography is not allowed inside the temple.

Opposite is **Dharmmikarama Burmese Buddhist Temple** (daily

Above: the 33-m (100-ft) reclining Buddha at Wat Chayamangkalaram

5am–6pm; free), Penang's first Buddhist temple, which houses a 8.3m (27ft) standing Buddha. Of note are two rows of smaller Buddha statues behind it, which are from different parts of the world. Once you have explored the inside of the temple, take a walk in the serene gardens, which are home to curiosities such as the World Guardian and Protector chimeras, a wishing pond set against a mural of the Great Renunciation of Prince Siddharta, and a floating shrine. A colourful time to visit these temples is the *Songkran* water festival in early April, but be prepared to get splashed.

Penang Botanic Gardens

From here, it's a 15-minute taxi ride to the **Penang Botanic Gardens** (daily 5am–8pm; free; www.sukpp.gov.my/KebunBunga/main.html). Ask your driver to wait while you explore the gardens, which will take about two hours. The 30-ha (72-acre) gardens nestled in the foothills of Penang Hill are the oldest and most well-maintained in Malaysia. Set up in 1884 as a nursery for the 'planting of colonial products', it was established to house botanic specimens from the surrounding hills, which were collected by its first superintendent.

Today, the mature, landscaped gardens comprise hundreds of trees and flowering plants from all over Malaysia and the tropics. There are also plant houses and nurseries, including a fern garden, a cactus house, orchid house and lily ponds. Animals, such as long-tailed macaques, monitor lizards and birds, are occasionally spotted – do not feed them. While some trees have labels, it is worthwhile buying a brochure of the gardens from **The Botanika** shop (daily 9am–1pm, 2–6pm; tel: 04-227 9915), which is located a short walk to the right of the entrance, on Lower Circular Road. Also sold at the shop are nature-based books and souvenirs, cold drinks and ice cream.

The gardens have three short walks on paved pathways – check out the map to the left, just inside the entrance gates. A recommended route is to go clockwise. When you hit Lower Circular Road, head towards the pretty Lily Pond and take the 15-minute jungle trek off that trail, the end of which rejoins Lower Circular Road. In May and June each year, an international floral festival is organised in the gardens, complete with displays, workshops and a floral parade. To the left of the entrance are a jeep path and a trail that go up to Penang Hill (*see Itinerary 4*).

Waterfall Road Temples

Next, make a stop at a couple of temples a five-minute drive away on Waterfall Road. The best time to visit them is from 5–5.30pm when a simple ceremony of bathing and unveiling the main statue takes place. On your left is a humble temple popularly known as the **Nattukottai Chettiar Hindu Temple** (daily; free). Consecrated in 1854, this temple undergoes a metamorphosis once a year during the Thaipusam festival, during which it virtually explodes into

Bottom left: Dharmmikarama Temple
Right: statue at Nattukottai Chettiar Hindu Temple

a spectacle of colour, sound and emotion. Otherwise, it quietly encapsulates the opulent if worn features of the once lucrative Chettiar network, such as chandeliers on teak beams, and intricate carvings and detailed paintings on the ceilings that were made by a Chettiar in Burma.

Opposite this temple is another one built by the Ayira Vaisyar, which is a small sub-ethnic group comprising mainly traders. Formerly dealers in recyclable material, they now deal in manufacturing, car components and textiles. Originally a community-cum-prayer hall, this temple is devoted to the group's patron saints, Meenachi and Siva, but it is unique in that almost every Hindu deity is represented here.

For a good Nonya dinner, take a taxi or a trishaw to Nagore Road. Located in a row of old shophouses that have now been converted into trendy eateries, **Nonya Baba Cuisine** (No 44; tel: 04-227 8035) has established a name for itself in the intriguing Malay-Chinese flavours of Straits Chinese food.

3. BATU FERRINGHI AND TELUK BAHANG
(see map, p18–19)

Check out Penang's famous beaches by spending all day lazing in the sun. Otherwise, find time for some souvenir shopping and a living spice museum. Either way, end the day with a stroll through a sidewalk bazaar.

Batu Ferringhi is 17km (10½miles) or about a 20-minute drive from Georgetown. Flag down a taxi (RM25) or hop on to Hin Bus 93 from Pengkalan Weld. For trekkers, the afternoon section of the tour can be replaced by a trek through Penang National Park (Itinerary 7).

Penang's beaches were responsible for the island's moniker of Pearl of the Orient. However, they have lost out to the island resorts of Langkawi and Peninsular Malaysia's east coast isles, where the waters are crystal clear, something impossible to achieve in developed Penang. Nonetheless, the beaches do not fare not too badly on the tropical isle barometer for relaxing and sunbathing, particularly after city-based heritage walkabouts. Watch out for jellyfish in the rainy season.

Batu Ferringhi Beach
The winding road from Georgetown to Teluk Bahang is dotted with public beaches equipped with food stalls, toilets and bathrooms. The main beaches

Above: parasailing fun at Batu Ferringhi beach
Top right: foot reflexology illustrated; **Bottom right:** Golden Sands Resort

on this stretch are **Tanjung Bungah**, **Batu Ferringhi** and **Teluk Bahang**. Of these, Batu Ferringhi is the liveliest, with eateries and restaurants from all over the world, cheap *batik* beachwear, Asian antiques and souvenirs, affordable tailors, moneychangers, travel agents offering transfers and trips elsewhere in the country as well as to Thailand, car and motorbike rentals, Internet cafés and hotels for every budget.

A Morning at the Beach

Start the day with a Continental or English breakfast with fresh juice at the homely, family-run **Kampung Restaurant** at 411 Batu Ferringhi (breakfast daily 8.30am–2pm; tel: 04-881 2676). After breakfast, cross the road, turn right and walk until you come to an access path to the beach. Sun seekers can easily laze away the morning on the beach. The more active can partake in water sports such as parasailing, jet skiing or banana-boat riding. Alternatively, treat yourself to reflexology, massage or palm reading.

You can also stroll along the beach, cooling down with an ice cream along the way as you take in the string of beachfront hotels and activities. The beach runs for 3km (1¼ miles) from the **Golden Sands Resort**, which sits to the right of the public beach access, and ends at the Bayview Beach Hotel. During the low tourist season, some hotels offer a day pass for the use of their facilities, such as the swimming pool and showers.

When you are beach-satiated, head up to the Tropical Spice Garden in

Teluk Bahang for lunch and a stroll in a garden. The journey should take about 20 minutes by taxi (RM10). The bus ride is longer, but stops right at the garden. If exploring Teluk Bahang, hire a taxi for four hours.

Tropical Spice Garden

The **Tropical Spice Garden** (daily 9am–6pm; admission charge; tel: 04-881 1797; www.tropicalspice garden.com) celebrates herbs and spices in the shape of more than 500 species of living plants, a museum and a shop. The **Tropical Spice Café** inside the gardens is a charming place. The menu may be small but it includes a hot main dish, a kid's menu, pies, pastries and desserts.

After lunch, walk up the steps to what was once a colonial holiday bungalow, and check out the gift shop. Continue on to the tiny museum, which presents a great historical overview of the lucrative spice trade and how it was instrumental in the formation and toppling of empires. Head back to the pavilion and walk off your lunch by spending an hour or so exploring this 2-ha (5-acre) landscaped area. If you prefer to have someone show you around, you can opt for a 45-minute guided tour (RM25).

Start with the **Ornamental Trail** with its water garden and giant swing, then go on to the **Spice Trail**, which showcases medicines, essential oils and dyes in their original form. The **Jungle Trail** is rather tame and rainforest aficionados will do better at the Botanic Gardens or Penang National Park.

Once you are done, you may want to take a dip in the ocean across the road. Otherwise, drive 10 minutes towards Teluk Bahang to reach the **Batik Factory** (daily 8.30am–5.30pm; tel: 04-885 1302), belonging to Craft Batik. The factory employs 50 locals from the Teluk Bahang village, who use stamping and hand-drawing methods to produce the *batik*.

Penang Butterfly Farm

The **Penang Butterfly Farm** (Mon–Fri 9am–5.30pm, weekends and public holidays 9am–6pm; admission charge; tel: 04-885 1253; www.butterfly-insect.com) is a five-minute drive up the Teluk Bahang road. The farm is home to 4,000–5,000 butterflies from 120 species, most of which are captive-bred. The **Insect and Reptile Show** (10am and 3pm) introduces various creatures, such as stick insects, snakes and water dragons, and children may feel them. Another fun feature is the **Hide-and-Seek Garden**, home to insects that are masters of camouflage.

Above: star anise; **Left:** the Penang Butterfly Farm has free-flying butterflies in an enormous enclosure; **Right:** the Night Market is an interesting shopping experience

Yahong Art Gallery

Head back now to Batu Ferringhi and go to the **Yahong Art Gallery** (daily 9.30am–10pm; free; tel: 04-881 1251), an established arts and craft centre and home to the paintings of Chuah Thean Teng. Chuah pioneered the use of traditional *batik* in artworks in the 1930s and his art has been compared to that of Matisse, Picasso and Gauguin. The gallery features his original pieces as well as works by his sons and other *batik* artists.

Batu Ferringhi Village and Night Market

From here, cross the road and turn left, walking until you come to a lane that will take you through the original **Batu Ferringhi village**. The lane curves to the right in a U-shape that rejoins the main road. The village still largely consists of the homes of the local fishermen, but some of the tiny houses have been turned into guesthouses. After passing Shalini's Guesthouse, you will see **Kompleks Bayu Senja**, which is probably the best seafront hawker centre in Batu Ferringhi; stop here for a cold drink or snack.

Go back to the main road and explore the rest of Batu Ferringhi. A good place to buy bargain *batik* is at the row of shops next to **Kampung Restaurant**. From pareos to sundresses, children's clothing, shirts and hats to artwork, the choice is huge. By 7pm, the **Night Market**, which stretches along the entire public roadside walkway in Batu Ferringhi, will have been set up. Here you get the gamut of fake branded products from leather handbags to Rolex watches, toys, trinkets, jewellery and T-shirts. Bargain hard.

For dinner, head back to Kompleks Bayu Senja for Chinese seafood at **Beach Corner** (daily 6.30–10.30pm). Fill up on its specialties of spring rolls, fried chicken, and fish and yam claypot, then wash it all down with cool, fresh coconut juice. Reservations are recommended on weekends.

penang itineraries

4. CENTRAL HILLS – AYER ITAM DAM, KEK LOK SI AND PENANG HILL *(see map, p18–19)*

Enjoy the fresh, early morning air at the island's biggest dam, then proceed to the impressive Kek Lok Si Temple and end at Penang Hill.

The attractions in this tour are in Ayer Itam, a small town about a 20-minute drive from Georgetown. Hire a taxi for the day, as taxis can be difficult to hail out of Ayer Itam. Buses to Ayer Itam are Transitlink 1 (from KOMTAR), Transitlink 91 and 92, and Penang Yellow Bus 79 (from the jetty). The route to Ayer Itam from Georgetown has heavy traffic during peak hours. The narrow roads in Ayer Itam see heavy traffic in the morning because of the market.

Ayer Itam Dam

This tour provides an experience of Penang's central hills. Because Penang is such a small island, it is important to protect its highland forests for water catchment. One of these catchment areas feeds into the island's largest dam, the **Ayer Itam Dam** (daily 6am–6pm), which is popular with walkers and joggers. Once you pass the market, a single road on the left, Jalan Buah Pala, wends its way up to the dam. On the right, just before the road starts climbing, is a century-old corner

Above: view of Ayer Itam Dam
Left: the winding road to the dam

penang itineraries

Hainanese coffeeshop called **Chop Wah Chee** (daily 8am–5pm). Run by fourth-generation coffeeshop operators, it is a great place to try excellent Thai-style *laksa*, which is a deliciously spicy and sour rice noodle dish, available here in three flavours – Thai, *asam* (spicy and sour), or a mix of the two. Have it with strong local black coffee.

From here, it is a 15-minute drive up a steep and winding road that exercise enthusiasts walk, jog or cycle up. This road ends at the dam. A fairly flat pedestrian road circles the dam and goes through rainforest; it takes about 40 minutes to complete. On this trail, you will see plants typical of the dipterocarp forest, such as tall trees with large buttress roots; woody lianas looped lazily over branches; and, on the moist ground, shrubs, ferns and orchids. Keep a sharp eye out for little lizards and skinks in the undergrowth, as well as birds, squirrels and monkeys in the treetops.

Kek Lok Si Temple Complex

When you are done, drive back down the hill and take the second of two right turnings. This will lead you to **Kek Lok Si** (daily 8am–6pm), a magnificent Buddhist temple complex. Allocate two hours for exploring this place, and ask your taxi driver to wait for you at the base of the hill at Chop Wah Chee *(see above)*. A good time to visit this temple is Chinese New Year, in late January or early February, when it is decorated with hundreds of lanterns.

Established in the late 19th century as a branch of the Buddhist 'Vatican' in Fujian, China, the Kek Lok Si complex is nestled on Crane Hill, so named because its founder saw, in the shape of the hills here, a crane with outspread wings. The crane is auspicious among Chinese as a symbol of wisdom, purity and high-mindedness. The simple monastery that was originally built here has grown in size and grandeur over the years.

Despite some commercialism, the Kek Lok Si is still considered one of Southeast Asia's most important temples. Inscriptions and endowments by China's Manchu Emperor and the Ching Dynasty Emperor and Empress form part of the temple's priceless artefacts. Of the temple's many halls, one important one is the **Hall of Devas**. Here stand large statues of the formidable looking Heavenly Kings, who control the universe at the four compass points. Under their hefty feet are various manifestations of evil: murderers, harlots, opium-smokers and liars. In contrast, the Laughing Buddha in the centre of the hall (representing the Universe) radiates prosperity and happiness.

Right: Kek Lok Si's Pagoda of Rama VI

Pagoda of Rama VI

Make your way up to the **Pagoda of Rama VI**, whose foundation stone was laid by the Thai monarch. A spiral staircase takes you up a heart-pumping seven storeys to views of the surrounding hills and of Ayer Itam. All the way up, the walls are decorated with alabaster and bronze Buddhas – 10,000 in all. What is interesting is that while the octagonal base of this pagoda is of Chinese design, the middle tiers are of Thai architectural style, and the crown is Burmese-inspired. This architectural mix reflects the temple's embracement of the two schools of Buddhism: Mahayana and Theravada.

Next, visit the 30-m (100-ft) bronze statue of **Greatly Compassionate and Sagely Kuan Yin Bodhisattva** (daily 8.30am–5.30pm; admission charge). Follow signs and get into the lift , which will take you to a spacious deck with great views of Georgetown. To the right is a serene garden in a gorgeous setting of verdant hills, one of which is the landmark Penang Hill. To the left you will see Kuan Yin with a bottle of holy water.

If you fancy an early lunch, there's a Chinese vegetarian restaurant (Mon–Fri 10am–7pm, weekends 10am–9pm) at the car park level where you were dropped off earlier. It has set meals here (rice and several dishes) or *a la carte* and is well known for its roasted 'chicken' in Szechuan spicy sauce as well as claypot noodle soup.

To finish your tour of the temple, take a different route down to the base of the hill by walking on the steps built over the old granite road, which was once the only access to the temple. Flanking it all the

Above: wall ornaments inside the Pagoda
Left: Kuan Yin; **Right:** rail to Penang Hill

way to the bottom are souvenir shops, where you can do some bargain shopping. When you have reached the bottom, refresh yourself at the Chop Wah Chee coffeeshop with freshly squeezed sugarcane or young coconut juice.

Penang Hill

Next, head to **Penang Hill**. A hill station established by Francis Light as Flagstaff Hill, it is accessible by funicular rail (daily 6.30am–9.45pm; admission charge), which takes 30 minutes to reach the upper station. The lower station is on Hill Railway Road, about 10 minutes by road from Kek Lok Si. However, what used to be its strongest selling point – its views – now has strong competition from the Kuan Yin statue level of Kek Lok Si. Moreover, during peak tourist periods, the queues to get onto the train are long. What Penang Hill does have going for it, though, is respite from the heat, since the air at its 735-m (2,410-ft) height is definitely cooler. There is also the 1.7-km (2.2-mile)-long **Canopy Walkway** (8.30am–5.30pm; free), from which vantage point you can see the tops of trees at leisure. Go slowly and pay attention to the shoots, young leaves, flowers and pollinating insects.

There is an asphalt jeep trail that goes down to the Penang Botanic Gardens (*see Itinerary 2*) and takes 1½ hours to tackle on foot. For jungle trekkers, there are in fact two trails that go up Penang Hill from the Botanic Gardens. These 7-km (4¼-mile) trails take four to five hours for the reasonably fit walker to complete. The first, 'traditional' trail offers great views and goes through the abandoned colonial Crag Hotel. The other is the heritage Moniot Road trail, which was built in the mid-1800s by Indian prisoners. It features points of interest from that time as well as colonial bungalows.

For maps of the trails, get the excellent Malaysian Nature Society's *Nature Trails of Penang Island* (*see Further Reading*) or download maps from the website, www.forestexplorers.com. However, it is advisable to hire a guide as some parts of the trails have changed or could be overgrown with foliage.

5. BATU MAUNG *(see map, p18–19)*

Drive down to the southeastern-most tip of the island for culture and history in the shape of a mysterious stone 'footprint' and a British fort.

This is a half-day tour that can be done in the morning or the afternoon. Hire a taxi for four hours. If you want to experience local colour, take the Penang Yellow Bus 68 or 69 from the jetty. The attractions in this itinerary are close enough to walk from one to the other. This tour can be combined with Itinerary 6 to make it a full-day drive around the island. In the latter case, you may want to consider hiring a car for the day.

From Georgetown, get onto the **Jelutong Expressway**, which will take you south all the way to Batu Maung – about 30 minutes if you do not stop. This is the best way of escaping Penang's nasty traffic, and you also get good views along this coastal road, which is built on reclaimed land.

Once you reach the Gelugor stretch before Penang Bridge, stop near the marine police pier – the marine police headquarters (Jabatan Laut Wilayah

Utara) are on the other side of the road. You get a good view of the **Penang Bridge** here.

Continue along this highway. You will soon see a large island on your left. This is **Pulau Jerejak**, once home to a leper hospital and a prison, and now an outward bound resort. To your right is the **Bayan Lepas Industrial Trade Zone**, established in 1970 and one of the largest electronics manufacturing bases in Asia. With high-tech electronic giants such as Intel, Agilent and Hitachi leading about 700 companies, manufacturing contributes to about 45 percent of the state's GDP. However, the manufacturing outlook is shaky because of competing lower labour costs in China, and Penang is therefore looking to reinvent itself.

Batu Maung Village

Leaving behind the steel and precision, you will arrive at a junction that is the start of **Batu Maung**, a small fishing village. Turn left and this will take you to the **Cheng Ho shrine**. This pretty Chinese temple pays tribute to the Chinese Columbus, Cheng Ho, an admiral who visited the Malay Peninsula in the 15th century, as a Goodwill Ambassador of the Ming Dynasty, on the first of his seven voyages to the Indian Ocean. It is to him that the local community attribute a recess in a rock in the shape of a giant footprint that the temple now enshrines. In reality, the footprint, measuring 85cm (33in),

Above: Cheng Ho's 'footprint'; **Top right:** Jacks and other deep-sea species are showcased in the Penang aquarium; **Bottom right:** entrance to the Penang War Museum

is unlikely to have belonged to the admiral, particularly as it has roots in the myths of various cultures. Indians believe it is the footprint of the great monkey god Hanuman. Local Malay folklore puts it down as the imprint left by a giant named Gedembai, who also left three other footprints – one on Penang island and two on Pulau Jerejak and Pulau Aman respectively. Gedembai also appears in the folklore of Langkawi. Whatever the case is, the 200-odd fishermen in the village whose lives and income depend on the ocean venerate this symbol, now synonymous with the great Chinese seafarer. The shrine looks out to the little jetty where bright blue fishing vessels are moored.

Fisheries Research Institute and Aquarium

Next on the itinerary is the **Fisheries Research Institute and Aquarium** (daily 10am–5pm, closed Wed; admission charge). To get there, head back to the junction but keep going straight, slowly, until you see the right turn into the institute. Turn into the carpark and head for the building on the left. A research facility set up for education, the aquarium is an informative introduction to the saltwater ecosystem and focuses on marine life, particularly corals from all over Malaysia. Of note are a touch tank where you can feel a sea cucumber and other harmless creatures, a giant tank featuring some very big fish, and, outdoors, a lovely corner displaying sea turtles of different ages.

War Museum

Your final stop is the **War Museum** (daily 9am–7pm; admission charge; tel: 04-626 5142). From the aquarium, drive back to the junction and turn

right. Once again, go slow to avoid missing the turn, and turn left when you see a tyre with the words 'Batu Maung Fort' written on it. The road winding up Bukit Batu Maung is steep and has deliberately been left in very bad shape, so be careful if you are driving.

A British Fort

The British built the fort in the 1930s in anticipation of World War II, thinking that invasions would come from the sea. Therefore, all canons, including a Howitzer monster gun and bunkers, were built for attack from that direction. When the Japanese did invade though, it was from land, and they practically strolled in. They seized Penang in six days, but the British in the fort managed to escape – to the sea – through a 30-m (100-ft) tunnel.

The Japanese used the fort as an interrogation centre for prisoners-of-war for the next two years. After the war, the fort was abandoned.

Finally, in 2000, the state government granted permission for a private company to convert the fort into a museum. The clearing of more than half a century of growth and debris revealed the fort to be in good shape, including the flooring and camouflage paintwork. Spread over 7.3ha (20 acres) and surrounded by peaceful lush rainforest, complete with chirping birds, the complex will take a couple of hours to explore.

Climb down long tunnels, marvel at the technology that allowed people to live underground, visit the operations centre, muse over the soldiers' segregated sleeping quarters, and observe the 1.5-m (5-ft)-thick walls and ceilings reinforced with cement, soil and steel. There are photographs, letters, newspaper cuttings and key documents on display, including personal memorabilia donated by former British soldiers. For a totally different experience, you might want consider touring this place at night for an additional fee. Museum staff can arrange pickups from hotels if you pay extra.

A Thai Lunch

When you are done, unwind with a Thai lunch in **Bukit Jambul** on the way back to Georgetown. Turn off the expressway at the Bandar Baru Bayan Baru intersection and follow the signs to the shopping mall. **Laempthong Restaurant** (lunch daily 12–2pm; tel: 012-475 2575), located opposite the mall at 6J–G Jalan Rumbia, features Phuket-style cooking. Try their specialties of seafood *otak-otak* in fresh coconut (a spicy prawn ensemble) and pineapple fried rice. There are also non-chilli variants.

Above: the grim exhibit of a Japanese torture chamber

6. RURAL PENANG
(see map, p18–19)

This is a scenic drive that takes you through the quiet agrarian parts of Penang. Along the way, stop at a Malay village and a small town, and drive through hilly orchards.

The starting point for this half-day tour is Batu Maung, so the tour can be combined with the previous itinerary. It ends in Teluk Bahang, so you could choose to explore the northern beaches and have dinner there (see Itinerary 3). This route is quite pleasant to drive yourself as the traffic is manageable. Alternatively, hire a taxi for half a day, but a surcharge may be imposed because of the distance.

Malay Villages

From Batu Maung, drive along Jalan Permatang Pauh towards Balik Pulau. You will pass **Malay *kampung*** (villages), which still comprise houses built in the traditional Malay architectural style, although this is fast changing in favour of the contemporary brick and tile. Well adapted to the hot tropical climate, Malay houses are made of wood and *attap* palm leaves, sit on stilts, and have triangular roofs from which rain water can flow off easily. The windows are large and reach to the floor, in order that occupants can easily see what is happening outside. Traditionally, there are few rooms, and families share the same space for everything, from sleeping and eating to hosting visitors. Likewise, neighbours are not separated by fences and it is common for children to wander in and out of each other's houses. Older members often gather in each other's compounds to catch up on news at day's end. Weddings and other rites of passage and festivals, such as Hari Raya, are celebrated communally.

Malay *kampung* are typically situated close to the main source of income, whether it be paddy fields, rubber or oil palm smallholdings, or the sea. A *kampung* would also have a common community hall, mosque or *surau* (prayer hall), cemetery, school and playing field.

Above: gleeful Malay boys
Right: a typical *kampung* house

Most *kampung* are open to a courteous request for a look-around. One village that is used to receiving visitors is **Kampung Seronok**, about 15 minutes' drive from Batu Maung. Look out for a signboard and a turning on the right. While the tide of modernity has left its mark on the village, communal living is still evident, and the villagers have taken care to preserve aspects of their heritage. The *kampung* adopted this name in the 1940s, after a visiting English engineer remarked on the felicity of communal celebrations – *seronok* translates as 'enjoy'. Ask for schoolteacher Cikgu Salleh, who can take you on a guided tour, or have a quick look around the community centre, cultural hall and traditional houses.

King of Fruits

Continue along and turn left once you reach the main road to go to Balik Pulau. This is a 12-km (7½-mile) drive in hilly terrain through rainforest and orchards. The soil on the island's west coast is conducive to the plant-

ing of fruit trees, and the most prized farms are those cultivating the Malaysian 'king of fruits' – the durian, a thorny fruit with a strong smell and taste. Because of its popularity, growing durian has become a real science, with hundreds of varieties cultivated, and quality fruit fetching high prices. The durian is seasonal, fruiting twice a year: May–July and November–January. There are stalls and farms along the road where you can sample the fruit.

Balik Pulau

Make a stop at **Balik Pulau**, a sleepy town where you will find excellent *laksa* (spicy rice noodle soup). To get to the eateries, head straight once you hit the roundabout. You will find a good *laksa* stall on this road outside the market and another in the corner coffeeshop to the right of the market. After your meal, return to the roundabout and take the road to **Batu Ferringhi**, 24km (15 miles) away. This is a pleasant drive through more Malay *kampung*, rainforest and orchards. After you hit Sungai Pinang, the road starts twisting and climbing as it moves into the central hills.

At the 11-km (6¾-mile) milestone, watch out for a sharp turn to the right that will take you to the **Tropical Fruit Farm** (daily 9am–6pm; admission charge; tel: 04-866 5186; www.tropicalfruits.com.my). The farm focuses on the conservation of fruit species and features over 200 types of tropical and sub-tropical fruits from all over the world. Take a guided farm tour, which lasts about an hour. The tour concludes with a fruit buffet. Alternatively, refresh yourself with fresh fruit juice at the farm's cafe, or try one of their local desserts.

After this break, get back onto the road and, in about 10 minutes, you will pass the **Teluk Bahang Dam**, which is the island's largest water supply project and the venue of the annual dragonboat race. Around the corner is Teluk Bahang, which is where this tour ends.

Above: the strong-smelling durian is usually not allowed into hotel rooms

7. COASTAL TREKKING *(see map below)*

Trek through the Penang National Park's coastal forest, enjoy secluded beaches and go up to the Muka Head lighthouse.

This tour consists of trekking one way and taking a boat back the other. The hike can be done in two parts: Teluk Bahang to the beach at Teluk Duyung, which takes over an hour, and Teluk Duyung to the Muka Head lighthouse, which takes an hour to ascend and half that time to descend. Set aside five hours for this tour. Before you begin, make arrangements at Teluk Bahang for a boatman to ferry you back (tel: 012-584 2265 [Rahim/Ah Chuan], 012-473 1299 [Atan], or 019-411 5143 [Shukri]). The boatmen are sometimes stationed at the Teluk Bahang jetty. Boats take 12 passengers and cost RM30 one way. Wear good walking shoes, bring insect repellent, bathers and sunblock, and pack a lunch complete with lots of water.

Experience a diversity of natural habitats in the **Penang National Park**, from coastal forest and rocky coastlines to beautiful sandy beaches. Covering 2,562ha (6,331 acres), the park comprises about 20 percent of the island's forest reserves and part of the catchment area for the Teluk Bahang Dam. The park is also Malaysia's only protected area under federal legislation (all other parks are under state laws) so it enjoys stronger protection.

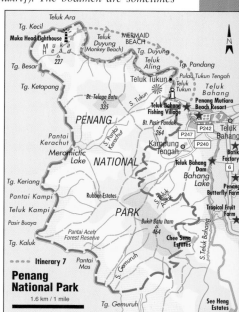

Penang National Park

1.6 km / 1 mile

Above: Penang National Park

Teluk Duyung Trail

There are several trails in this park. The well-marked **Teluk Duyung trail**, which is 2.6km (1.6 miles) long, is the most popular and is fairly easy. Commonly known as the trail to Muka Head or Monkey Beach, it has long been used by locals, in particular boy scouts, army reservists and anglers. How-

ever, it is now more accessible to the public in its incarnation as a National Park trail, as bridges and steps have been built over the trickier terrain, and more information has been put up, including labels on trees. The trail can be crowded on weekends. As you walk, enjoy the sound of waves, take note of the vegetation and terrain, and look out for fauna such as squirrels, monkeys, lizards, monitor lizards, pretty butterflies and hosts of birds.

The start of the trail is at **Teluk Bahang** village. You may want to fortify yourself here with a good breakfast before the trek. **Restoran Ibrahim** to the left of the main road before the roundabout serves crispy *roti*, a buttery Indian bread, which goes well with *dhal*. You can also get them to pack you a lunch of *mee goreng* (fried noodles).

After breakfast, drive to the fishing jetty. Sign in at the **park headquarters** (Mon–Fri 8am–4.30pm, weekends 8am–12pm, 2–4pm) and grab a map. There is a 24-hour grocery store here in case you need to stock up on snacks and drinks. The trail is to the left of the jetty. A tree you will often encounter as you hike along is the Pelawan (Eugenia) with its bright red trunk of sometimes peeling bark; this tree is related to the Australian Eucalyptus. Because this area is near the coast, the trees are not very large.

After about 10 minutes, you will arrive at **Teluk Tukun**, where there are some abandoned chalets but usable toilets. Take a 10-minute detour to the left here to go up to a lookout. Look out for the mangrove trees along the river.

Beach Stops

Back on the main trail, it will take about 20 minutes to reach **Teluk Aling**, the next bay and the site of a university research station. The beach here is lovely and you might want to take a dip in the sea to cool off. The trail continues along the beach, and later goes into the forest. From here, you will need to walk for 30–40 minutes to reach the final stop. This stretch of the trail is hilly, but you can take a break at a rest area at the halfway point. You will see some larger trees with big buttress roots here.

Above: start of the Teluk Duyung trail; **Top right:** trail to the Muka Head lighthouse
Bottom right: the Muka Head lighthouse stands at only 143m (470ft) tall

Teluk Duyung

Finally, you'll see steps leading down to **Teluk Duyung**. Stretching for about 1km (½ mile) and lined by coconut trees, casuarinas and shady sea almond trees, this beach is wonderful for relaxing, sunbathing and swimming. Behind the beach spreads a former coconut plantation and a carpet of tall grass through which you might catch sight of the twitching tail of one of the many long-tailed macaques that give this place its popular moniker, Monkey Beach. Look up and you are likely to see majestic White-bellied Sea Eagles in the sky.

Muka Head Lighthouse

For those who are up to a climb, walk to the end of the beach past two abandoned bungalows, then continue uphill for about 1¼km (¾ mile) until you arrive at the **Muka Head lighthouse**. This structure, built in 1883, is closed to the public, but the keeper sometimes lets visitors in. The trail up goes through thicker forest where wildlife abounds. Look out for a species of hard-to-spot pitcher plants between the 0.7km and 0.8km marker stones.

Going down the hill is much quicker. Taking the boat back to the jetty is a pleasant 20-minute ride and gives you a different view of the park.

penang itineraries

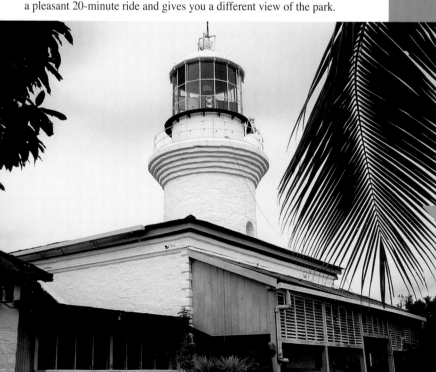

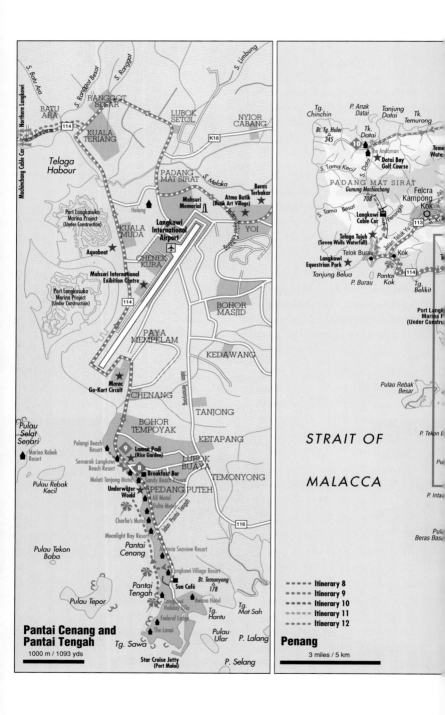

Pantai Cenang and Pantai Tengah
1000 m / 1093 yds

Penang
3 miles / 5 km

- - - - Itinerary 8
- - - - Itinerary 9
- - - - Itinerary 10
- - - - Itinerary 11
- - - - Itinerary 12

STRAIT OF

MALACCA

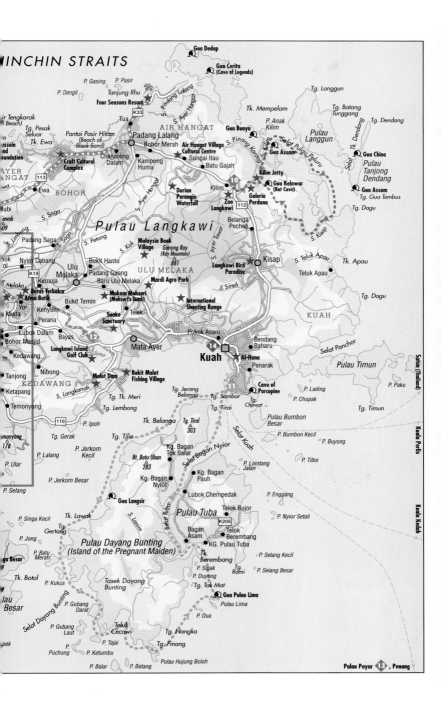

INCHIN STRAITS

Gua Dedap

Gua Cerita
(Cave of Legends)

P. Gasing   P. Pasir
P. Dangli   Tanjung Rhu
Four Seasons Resort
Tk. Mempelam
Tg. Langgun
Tg. Batang
Tunggang
Tg. Dendang
Tua
K33
AIR HANGAT
Gua Buaya
P. Anak
Kilim
Pulau
Langgun
Tk. Dendang
r Tengkorak
ll Beach)
Tg. Pesak
Seluar
Tk. Ewa
Pantai Pasir Hitam
(Beach of
Black Sand)
Padang Lalang
Bohor Merah
Air Hangat Village
Cultural Centre
Sungai Itau
Batu Gajah
Kilim
Gua Assam
Selat Pulau Peluru
Gua China
Pulau
Tanjong
Dendang
ssein
nd
undation
Chenarong
Dalam
Kampong
Huma
Kilim Jetty
AYER
ANGAT
113
Ewa
BOHOR
Craft Cultural
Complex
Durian
Perangin
Waterfall
Kilim
Zoo
Langkawi
112
10
Galeria
Perdana
Gua Kelawar
(Bat Cave)
Gua Assam
Tg. Gua Tembus
Tg. Dagu
ubi
awak
09
S. Soga
Padang Saga
S. Limbing
S. Soga
Pulau Langkawi
Belanga
Pechah
S. Petang
S. Kok
Malaysia Book
Village
Gunung Ray
(Ray Mountain)
881
Langkawi Bird
Paradise
Kisap
S. Teluk Apau
Tk. Apau
ol
K18
Nyior Cabang
Ulu
Melaka
Bukit Hantu
ULU MELAKA
Teluk Apau
Tg. Dagu
Kemoja
Padang Gaong
Baru Ulu Melaka
Mardi Agro Park
S. Sireh
KUAH
S. Melaka
Beras Terbakar
Atma Batik
Yoi
Muda
Kenyum
Perana
Bukit Temin
Makam Mahsuri
(Mahsuri's Tomb)
International
Shooting Range
Snake
Sanctuary
Telek
Lubok Dalam
Bayas
12
Mata Ayer
Pokok Asam
14
Kuah
Al-Hana
Bendang
Baharu
Selat Panchor
Pulau Timun
Satun (Thailand)
Bohor Masjid
Langkawi Island
Golf Club
Kedawang
KEDAWANG
Nibong
Malut Dam
Bukit Malut
Fishing Village
Penarak
Cave of
Porcupine
P. Lading
P. Paku
Tanjong
Ketapang
S. Langkanah
Tg. Tk. Meri
Tg. Jerang
Belanga
Tg. Sambar
Tg. Tirai
Tg.
Chawat
P. Chupak
Kuala Perlis
Temonyong
116
P. Ipoh
Tg. Lembong
Tk. Belanga
Tg. Tiral
303
Pulau Bumbon
Besar
P. Bumbon Kecil
P. Buyong
Tg. Timun
monyong
178
Tg. Gerak
P. Jerkom
Kecil
Tg. Tilin
Kg. Bagan
Tok Safar
Selat Bogan Nyior
Selat Kuah
P. Tilloi
Kuala Kedah
P. Lalang
P. Ular
Bt. Batu Uban
283
Kg. Bagan
Nyior
Kg. Bagan
Pauh
P. Lointang
Jalan
P. Selang
P. Jerkom Besar
Gua Langsir
Lubok Chempedak
Telok Bujor
P. Enggang
P. Nyior Setali
P. Singa Kecil
Tk. Lawak
Pulau Tuba
K205
Tg.
Gertang
P. Jong
S. Lamin
S. Tuba
Bagan
Asam
Telok
Berembang
KG. Pulau Tuba
P. Batu
Merah
Pulau Dayang Bunting
(Island of the Pregnant Maiden)
Tk.
Berembang
P. Selang Kecil
a Besar
P. Sipak
P. Duyong
Tg.
Rami
P. Selang Besar
Tk. Botol
P. Kukus
Tasek Dayang
Bunting
Tg. Tok Mat
Gua Pulau Lima
au
Besar
P. Gubang
Darat
Teluk
Cecawi
Pulau Lima
P. Dua
P. Gubang
Laut
Selat Dayang Bunting
pek
P. Tajai
Tg. Nangka
Puchong
P. Ketumbu
Tg. Pinang
P. Balar
P. Batang
Pulau Hujung Boloh
Palau Payar
13
, Penang

Langkawi
Itineraries

Langkawi is an archipelago of 99 islands covering 478sq km (185sq miles) northeast of the Peninsula and north of Penang, near the Thai border. Belonging to the state of Kedah, Langkawi is actually the name of the main island, which stretches 25km (15½ miles) from north to south and slightly more from east to west. This is where the infrastructure, tourist facilities and the international airport are located. Only a few other islands are inhabited but getting around by boat is easy.

Langkawi's draw is the natural beauty of its many islands, fascinating geological landscapes, including the oldest rock in Malaysia, a million-year-old rainforest, gorgeous sandy beaches as well as pretty coral reefs. Legends also colour this archipelago, with a story behind almost every place name, whether it be an island or a mountain or beach.

Half the terrain comprises dramatic highlands and forest, and the other half, rustic villages and paddy fields. The main town is Kuah in the southeast, which is the commercial and banking area, and where boats to the mainland depart and arrive. There is some tourist accommodation here but no beach. The beaches and main tourist stretches are in the west of the island at Pantai Cenang, Pantai Tengah and Pantai Kok; and in the north, at Teluk Datai and Tanjung Rhu, where the luxury hotels can be found.

The pace is slow and leisurely in Langkawi. In the first three days, a series of half- and full-day itineraries will have you relaxing on beautiful beaches and going up an ancient mountain to see what the earth was like 500 million years ago. Learn about the different ecosystems that make up the rainforest, and take a boat out to fully grasp the island geography and the vastness of this archipelago.

If you are spending more time in Langkawi, the next four itineraries guide you as you explore more of the island to appreciate its agrarian sensibilities; go underwater to see the coral reefs of Pulau Payar; and shop for souvenirs in Kuah before going on a sunset cruise just before nightfall.

Driving is safe and easy in Langkawi and car hire is cheap. There are plenty of taxis, but the best bet is to hire a car for the duration of your stay. Taking tours with nature guides is also imperative for fully appreciating Langkawi. Likewise, boating and yachting allow you to really grasp the magnitude of archipelago. There is a range of nature-based activities for all interests and capabilities, but the minimum you should do is a rainforest interpretative tour.

Left: Langkawi is about being laid-back
Right: a Malay youth

8. PANTAI CENANG AND PANTAI TENGAH
(see map, p48–49)

Spend your morning enjoying Langkawi's beautiful beaches and learning about the marine environment.

This half-day itinerary begins at the northern end of Pantai Cenang and ends in Pantai Tengah in the south. Although this is recommended as a walking tour, it can also be accomplished by bicycle. This morning trip can be combined with Itinerary 9 to make a full-day tour.

Lined with cafés, eateries, hotels and souvenir shops, **Pantai Cenang** is the island's liveliest beach – but only from 11am, for here, as elsewhere in Langkawi, things start off leisurely and late. Begin your day with a local *roti canai* (South Indian bread) breakfast at the **Breakfast Bar** (daily 7am–2pm).

After your meal, cross the road and head to the beach, which is a coconut palm-fringed sandy stretch of about 2km (1½ miles) long that slopes gently into a calm expanse of warm blue sea. Anywhere along this beach is perfect for sunbathing, swimming and cooling down with fresh fruit juice. Watersports such as kayaking, jet skiing and parasailing are also available. For something more low key, try foot reflexology or a relaxing massage, all while enjoying the soft sounds of the gentle surf.

Underwater World Langkawi

Take a nice beach walk from the **Pelangi Beach and Spa Resort** to the Underwater World in about a quarter of an hour. The sprawling Pelangi created a stir 16 years ago as one of the first four-star Malay *kampung* or village-style resorts to be built while the rest of Cenang was jungle. Today the sizable hotel is popular with everyone, from dignitaries to families.

Heading south along the beach after the Pelangi, you will pass a range of accommodation. This used to be a backpacker stretch, but the hotels in this area are gradually going upmarket. Cafés worth stopping at are the **Beach Garden Resort Bistro** (8am–10.30pm; tel: 04-955 1363) at the northern end,

and the **Red Tomato Splash Beach Café** (9am–10pm; tel: 04-955 3088). Both have a lovely ambience, especially if a sea breeze is blowing, and serve fresh juices, coffees, beers and snacks.

Once you have passed the Desa Motel, make a left turn towards the road so that you will arrive at **Underwater World Langkawi** (daily 10am–6pm; admission charge; tel: 04-955 6100). This is home to Malaysia's largest collection of aquatic life, with more than 500 species of creatures and coral species in 115 tanks.

You can easily spend two hours at this attraction, moving from a tropical ecosystem to temperate and sub-Antarc-

Left: penguins at Underwater World Langkawi

tic displays, and finally ending at the aquarium-only section. A well-conceived design and careful landscaping make for a lush tropical ecosystem section, which comes complete with free-flying birds and Amazonian creatures such as anaconda and piranha.

The **penguin feeding sessions** in the temperate (10.30am and 3pm) and sub-Antarctic sections (11am and 3.30pm) are fun to watch. The long marine tunnel in the aquarium section has marine goliaths like leopard sharks and manta rays swimming overhead as you walk. An informative seven-minute screening of marine life plays every hour in the 3D Theatre. While the Underwater World is easy enough to wander around by yourself, you may wish to join a 90-minute guided tour of the aquarium – ask at the information counter. Note that this attraction gets very crowded during school holidays.

Pantai Tengah Beach

From here, head to **Pantai Tengah** in the south by walking along the road. Shops will be opening by now. At the T-junction, turn right and then left into Jalan Teluk Baru. Pantai Tengah used to comprise a handful of well-spaced hotels along the beach, but recent years have seen a southward migration of Pantai Cenang's tourist traps. However, there is a concerted effort – business rather than government-led – to manage the development here. The idea is to create an entertainment hub that is more organised and upmarket.

A sign of things to come is the **Sun Café** (daily noon–midnight; tel: 04-9558 300) at Shop No 8 Sunmall, a great place to lunch. A classy, modern eatery with a European feel, its emphasis is on fresh and homemade ingredients. Try its thin-crust pizzas and sandwiches. The owners also built the restaurant complex opposite and have plans for more projects on the same stretch.

After lunch, head through the **Langkawi Village Resort** – the entrance is diagonally across the road from Sun Café – for the long stretch of white sand beach at Pantai Tengah. The resort is set to become a four-star boutique hotel and spa by late 2006. Enjoy your afternoon at the nice beach bar here.

Above: the Sun Café serves great pizzas
Right: view at Langkawi Village Resort

9. CABLE CAR AND MACHINCHANG *(see map, p48–49)*

Go on a cable car ride for spectacular views and come face to face with the oldest rock in Malaysia.

This tour can be done in the afternoon in combination with the previous itinerary. Hire a taxi for half a day. The journey from Pantai Cenang to the cable car station takes about half an hour. Set aside at least two hours for this tour, more if you want to spend time at the nearby Pantai Kok beach. An interpretive guide will enrich your experience.

From the bustle of Pantai Cenang, you drive north through the sort of terrain that makes this resort island so relaxing – first, ocean, then, small towns and fishing villages before thick, hilly forest takes over. Along the way, there is unfortunate dissonance at the Telaga Harbour development, a French Riviera-style marina project that occupies what was once a beautiful sweep of beach. Other than that, it is a lovely drive to one of the island's top draws.

The Machinchang Formation

The base station of the **Langkawi Cable Car** (Mon, Tue, Thur 10am–6pm, Wed 12pm–6pm, Fri–Sun and public holidays 9.30am–7pm; admission charge; tel: 04-959 4225) is in the Oriental Village, a tourist attraction that never took off. Covering a distance of over 2km (1½ miles) and going up to 708m (2,323ft) above sea level, the cable car ride offers breathtaking views of the Langkawi archipelago, mainland Peninsular Malaysia and even South Thailand. Call beforehand to ensure the service is not closed, whether it be for maintenance or because the weather is too stormy, windy or foggy – the latter is a strong likelihood between mid-August and November.

From the base station, it is a 14-minute ride to the top, with a brief stop at mid-station. Spread out below you are the Bukit Sawak and Gunung Machinchang Forest Reserves, comprising the richly diverse vegetation and tall trees of the lowlands that gradually give way, as you climb, to lower diversity and shorter, hardier plants. As the panorama begins to unfold, look out for the Telaga Tujuh waterfall. The wonderful forest sits on rocks that were formed 550 million years ago when sand deposits initiated the historical geological process that became the landmass now called Malaysia.

This is the **Machinchang Formation**, consisting of layers of sandstone, conglomerate, siltstone and mudstone and characterised by rugged mountain peaks and very steep to vertical cliffs.

At the top, enjoy the amazing landscape from two beautifully-designed viewing platforms. At the steps of the second viewing platform, look out for the geological showcase of wave ripple marks on sandstone. This monumental mountain was once an ancient seabed, thrust upwards by the power of earth's forces.

There is also a spectacular 200-m (656-ft)-long suspension bridge that takes you to more views. Alternatively, take the 20-minute trail beneath the bridge to get to the other end. This trail goes through beautiful red-barked *kelat bukit* (Syzigium species) forest.

Telaga Tujuh Waterfall

An alternative to the cable car is the walk up **Telaga Tujuh** or Seven Wells, a seven-step waterfall believed in myth to be the playground of fairies. A special kind of lime and root found in this area, which locals used as a shampoo in the past, is believed to have been left by these fairies. The base of the waterfall is a quick drive up the road from the cable car station, and walking up to the topmost pool involves climbing 638 steps. The best time to see this waterfall in full flow is the rainy season between August and November. Pack swimming gear and a picnic to make a nice event of the tour.

Pantai Kok Beach

Next, spend time enjoying the **Pantai Kok beach**. Head to the **Mutiara Burau Bay Beach Resort** and look for a nice spot on the beach. You can also rent watersports equipment here and enjoy drinks and snacks from the resort's bars.

For some horse riding, drive through the resort to the end of the road to reach the **Langkawi Equestrian Park** (daily 8–11.30am, 3–7pm; tel: 019-437 9783 [Hamzah]). The park has 13 horses, all former racehorses and five trainer/guides. You can choose a beach or jungle trail, or a combination of both; rides last between a half hour to two hours.

For dinner, head back to Pantai Cenang. Dine on excellent Western food with a twist of Malaysian at the **Bon Ton Restaurant and Resort** (daily dinner 7–11pm; tel: 04-955 3643). After your meal, you can also have a look at the lovely resort, which is made up of 100-year-old Malay houses.

eft: gorgeous views from a cable car station
bove: bridge over magnificent forest reserves; **Right:** Telaga Tujuh

10. EXPERIENCING THE RAINFOREST *(see map, p48–49)*

Start the day with a dawn walk in the rainforest, then take a boat ride through a beautiful mangrove area, and visit a bat cave.

This is a rainforest discovery itinerary. It will take you through two types of ecosystems – a mixed dipterocarp forest and a mangrove forest in northern Langkawi. This itinerary actually comprises two tours offered by nature tour operators, but you can either ask for them to be combined as one, or use two separate agencies. Operators usually do pick-ups from your hotel. Set aside five to six hours for this itinerary. Make sure you select a good interpretive nature guide who will be responsible enough to not engage in eagle feeding, which has become popular in Kilim – feeding changes the birds' habits and can lead to deformed chicks. A responsible guide will also travel slowly along the river to avoid creating waves, which slowly erode the mangroves and limestone. Be sure to take insect repellent with you.

Dipterocarp Rainforest Tour

Dawn is one of the best times to appreciate the rainforest, as this is when birds and other creatures are most active, and the freshly dew-soaked forest is beautiful in the soft light. It is also cooler to walk at this time.

The foothills of the Machinchang range on the side of The Datai hotel are a good place to get acquainted with the mixed dipterocarp forest, as you can walk on a tarred road that does not have heavy traffic and which is bordered by primary rainforest. This tour was developed by Langkawi naturalist Irshad Mubarak for hotel guests of The Datai, but now other guides use it too.

Start your walk at about 7.30am. Since you never know what you are going to run across when it comes to wildlife, there is no typical tour experience. It could be a short trek of a few hundred metres where you encounter plenty of birds, which is likely during the migratory season from October

to April, or a 2-km (1½-mile) stroll in which you learn mainly about the forest's large diversity of plants.

Walking on the road gives you a different experience from trekking in the thick forest as you are able to see a vertical dissection of the various layers of the rainforest. On the forest floor, look out for fungi and trails of ants. At the shrub layer, what look like garden weeds might have the most unexpected uses for humans in traditional healing. High up in the canopy, see how competition for sunlight shapes the crowns of trees. The largest trees are likely to be dipterocarps, the dominant family of trees in this forest. There are also semi-evergreen or deciduous trees here, which shed their

Left: dipterocarp forests typically consist of rainforest trees with two-winged fruits

leaves not during winter but during the distinct dry season at the end of the year.

Kilim

To experience another equally fascinating ecosystem, head on to **Kilim**, where there are extensive mangroves and beautiful limestone landscapes, for a boat tour. The trip usually takes three hours, and much of it will be on **Kilim river**, which gained worldwide exposure – but not fame since it was never identified – in the closing scenes of the Hollywood production, *Anna and the King.*

As you drift along, you will see how water has been patiently shaping this 300-million-year-old limestone formation. A combination of wave and rainwater action has resulted in a rugged landscape comprising irregular cliffs, rounded domes and exposed grey limestone.

It is on limestone substrate that the mangroves grow. In fact, Langkawi is the only place in Malaysia where you find this combination of vegetation, rocks and soil type. Mangroves are unique plants that grow in the area between land and sea, an environment that is alternately wet and dry, which is why they are found only on coasts. They play key roles in preventing coastal erosion and act as a natural breakwater against storms. They are also important breeding and feeding grounds for fisheries.

Certain species of mangrove wood also make the best charcoal. Once a thriving industry here, the managed harvesting and conversion of mangrove wood to charcoal is slowly dying out. Today, there is only one active kiln remaining, and it is well worth stopping at for an insight into traditional charcoal processing.

Gua Kelawar and Selat Peluru

The tour includes a visit to one of many caves that can be found in the Kilim area, **Gua Kelawar**. Otherwise known as Bat Cave, it is home to Malaysian fruit bats, which hang upside down on the ceiling by day and fly out to feed at night. Look out for old shells on the cave walls and roof. These fossils are about 5,000 years old, remnants of a time when the sea level was 2–5m (7–16ft) higher than it is today.

The tour should also include a ride into **Selat Peluru**, the straits between Langkawi and its neighbouring islands. Look out for dolphins here. Coming from the sea into the limestone-lined Kilim river is a lovely sight. This passage, which has been quirkily dubbed the Hole in the Wall, is also popular with yachties.

Above: stilt roots of the mangrove
Right: a traditional charcoal kiln

11. ISLAND HOPPING *(see map, p48–49)*

Take a speedboat tour of several islands, chill out at a secluded beach, and come up close and personal with amazing seascapes.

A variety of island-hopping tours is available. This tour takes you to one of the most visited islands, but it does not follow the standard tour format. You will need to tell your boatman where you want to go. The trip is best done in the morning and takes four hours, most of which will be spent on a speedboat. The sea can be choppy after a rainy night. Regardless of the weather, be prepared to get wet, so be sure to waterproof your camera and other items that you want to keep dry. Bring swimming gear, sunblock and an

extra change of clothes. Drinks are usually provided and you can ask for a picnic to be packed for an additional charge; otherwise get your hotel to pack you a lunch. This itinerary leaves from the main jetty in Kuah next to the Royal Langkawi Yacht Club, where most of the island-hopping tours depart. Boat hire prices range from RM350–500 per boat, which can take up to six passengers. You can also start your island-hopping tour from the other beaches on the island.

This tour gives you a feel for the size of the Langkawi archipelago and its many islands, big and small.

Above: pregnant maiden profile
Left: timeless rock features

Pulau Dayang Bunting

A large part of the tour takes place around **Pulau Dayang Bunting** (Island of the Pregnant Maiden), which is the second largest island after Langkawi island. The former island is best known for a lake located in its southwestern part, and the place is well known for two reasons.

The first is a famous myth, of which there are several versions, all of which are centred around a lady-in-waiting who became pregnant after drinking from this lake. That the lake aids in conceiving has come to be regarded as truth by locals. The fact that the undulating hills do, from a certain angle, resemble a woman in a childbearing posture lends support to the age-old legend.

The second reason is a natural mystery as the lake holds freshwater despite there being an opening between the lake and the sea. The lake was probably formed long ago when an underground limestone cave collapsed. In fact, limestone is what accounts for the dramatic landscapes of Dayang Bunting; the limestone here is of the same age as that in Kilim (*see Itinerary 10*).

Departing on your island hopping from Kuah in the morning gives you the chance to see how the shadows gradually lift from the hills as the sun rises in the sky. As you travel along the western side of Dayang Bunting, the round-topped limestone hills rise almost vertically from the ground – very steep terrain is a feature of the western and southern sides of this island.

Gua Langsir

About 20 minutes after you depart, look out for a cave opening high up in the rockface of a 90-m (295-ft) hill. Partly obscured by thick vegetation, this is **Gua Langsir**, named after the *langsir*, a vampire-type female spirit believed to be the source of the strange sounds emitting from the cave. Other more identifiable sounds – clicking, buzzing and high-pitched squeaks – are that of the thousands of bats that call it home.

As you ride along, you are likely to encounter an age-old scene – colourful fishing boats moored in a bay while fishermen and women in large hats cast or pull up their nets. These people you see are either Burmese folk from the several-thousand strong fishing community on Langkawi island, or Thai fishermen hired by fishing fleet operators in Perlis or the Kedah mainland. For them and the generations of fishermen before them, the islands have provided sustenance and a safe haven from storms and pirates.

Modern-day fisheries have also made the most of the nutrient-rich waters here, and you will see government-run fish farms. The fish from these farms are expensive species farmed for the export market. From around the vantage point of an island here called **Batu Merah**, you will be able to perceive the shape of the pregnant maiden on Dayang Bunting formed by the hills.

Close to this area is the jetty to

Right: Thai-manned fishing boats in sheltered bays

the lake, which, unfortunately, has become rather commercialised – jet skis and all – and can be rather crowded. However, the 10-minute trail walk is worth it for an opportunity to get close-up views of the beautiful limestone and its vegetation. Be careful of the aggressive monkeys: make sure all food is securely packed and placed out of sight.

Teluk Cecawi and Gua Pulau Lima

From here, it is a five-minute boat ride to **Teluk Cecawi**, a small, beautiful and secluded beach of white sand in the south of the island. Spend time here chilling out – swimming in the blue waters, having a picnic and catching some sun. As you continue on your journey, you will pass through the narrow straits before hitting the open ocean. The waves will be stronger here, and in about 10 minutes, you will reach the amazing rock formations of **Pulau Lima**, so named because it is a cluster of five islands.

This island group provides a macro view of how layer upon layer of sediments were deposited when the area was a wide but shallow sea millions of years ago. These bedding planes mark periods during which no deposits took place and each layer therefore might be made up of different compositions. Over time, these layers became buried and started turning into rocks through compaction and cementing. The whole area was uplifted, and finally, weather and waves resulted in what you see here.

Among Pulau Lima's features are sea arches, formed when erosion wiped out the weaker layers, leaving only the harder beds. There is even a palaeo sea arch high on one of the islands, indicating the former sea level.

Head towards **Gua Pulau Lima**, a lovely little sea cave formed when waves attacked zones of weakness in the cliff. Note the stalactites hanging down, white calcite deposit stains, rust-colour iron stains and marine shell deposits on the walls. There is life here too – bats snooze from the ceiling and swallows build their nests in any nook or cranny. Look out for a large

eagle's nest on a tree near the sea arch. To the left of this cave, scour the cliff wall and you will see a vertical garden of cycads, the world's oldest seed plant. These palm-like plants are sometimes called *belalai gajah* (elephant trunks) – or *bogak* in local parlance.

From here, head back to Kuah through **Selat Tuba**, which is the scenic straits between Dayang Bunting and Pulau Tuba. This passage, which will take approximately 20 minutes to navigate, is lined with mangrove trees growing on flat muddy beaches; the latter are frequently inundated by the tides. There are also several fishing villages along the way.

Left: the aptly named *belalai gajah*

12. Scenic Drive *(see map, p48–49)*

Soak in laid-back Langkawi on this all-day drive, indulge in a spa treatment and end the day by enjoying a spectacular sunset.

This drive goes through central and northern Langkawi and takes about six hours; make sure you time it for the sunset. You could hire a car for the day or have a driver take you. If you are visiting the Ibrahim Hussein Museum and Cultural Foundation (tel: 04-959 4669) or The Spa (tel: 04-959 2500), make sure you ring up a couple of days beforehand to make an appointment. Pack your swimmers in case you want to go into the ocean. Your starting point is the Siti Fatimah restaurant on Jalan Kampung Tok Senik, the road to Makam Mahsuri, which is about 20 minutes by road from Kuah and 30 minutes from Pantai Cenang.

Start off with a *kampung* or village-style Malay meal at **Restoran Siti Fatimah** (daily 7am–11pm, closed Wed; tel: 04-955 2754) at 5¼ Mile, Jalan Kampung Tok Senik. From here, the roads wind lazily through paddy fields and villages laid out against the mountains of the lushly forested **Bukit Sawak Forest Reserve**.

Makam Mahsuri

Leaving from the restaurant, turn right towards Ulu Melaka. You will pass a turning on your right to **Makam Mahsuri**, or Mahsuri's Tomb. Unfortunately, the place has been commercialised and is worth visiting perhaps only for legend aficionados. After the 3-km (1¾-mile) mark, make a right turn, and then turn left at the T-junction. Drive for another 7½ km (4¾ miles), and enjoy the distinctly Malay rural environment.

Above: an idyllic sunset view from Tanjung Rhu beach
Right: a verdant Malaysian landscape

A Batik Art Village

When you come to a junction, turn right and after 1.6km (1 mile) there are vast paddy fields and a Petronas petrol station. **Atma Batik** (daily 9am–6pm; tel: 04-955 2615), or Batik Art Village, is opposite the station. Here, you can watch a short *batik*-making demonstration, during which wax is drawn on material using a *canting*, a wooden 'pen'. You can also try your hand at producing your own *batik* masterpiece (classes daily except Fri, 2pm). There is also a large shop and gallery where you can purchase *batik* cloth as well as souvenirs from throughout Asia.

Continue with the drive by taking a right turn back onto the road. At the traffic lights, turn right again into Jalan Kuala Teriang, which goes through **Padang Matsirat** town where there is a lively market until noon. After about 7km (4 miles), turn right at the junction at **Kuala Teriang village** to take the lovely hilly road for 13½km (8½ miles) that leads to the cable car (*Itinerary 9*). After Telaga Harbour, turn right into Jalan Teluk Yu to get to the northern part of the island.

On this stretch of road, human habitation thins out and rubber estates and rainforest take over. Drive for about 4km (2½ miles) until you come to a left turn into Jalan Datai, which goes to the northwest corner of the island. From this road, you get beautiful vistas of islands and ocean, and the Machinchang forest and geology. This is also where the luxury hotels are located.

Stop at the **Ibrahim Hussein Museum and Cultural Foundation** (daily 10am–6pm; admission charge; tel: 04-959 4669; www.ihmcf.org), a beautiful art gallery located in the forest, owned and run by one of Malaysia's foremost abstract artists. Allocate at least an hour for this museum of stunning architecture, expansive views and exceptional artwork.

Beach, Rock Formations and Waterfalls

Next to the museum is a lovely public beach with clear water and white sand (and a name that does it no justice): **Pantai Pasir Tengkorak** (Sandy Skull Beach). You may want to take a dip in the sea. Otherwise, explore the beautiful geological formations of ancient rock by walking a short distance to the right to **Tanjung Buta**. Here, you will see the large-scale result of erosion millions of years ago. Beds of sediment deposits that make up sandstone are normally layered horizontally. However, here on sandstone that is more than 1m (3ft) thick, the beds are tilted at different angles to each other. More recent weathering has left interesting honeycomb patterns on the rock.

The near-vertical cliffs of the Machinchang Formation also make for gorgeous waterfalls, one of which sits just down the road. The 300-m (100-ft) **Temurun Waterfall** is only a waterfall six months a year, during the rainy season. When it is in full flow, it is quite an inspiring sight.

Above: colour being applied to a *batik* design at Atma Batik

Spa Treatments

When you are done, indulge yourself with a massage at the award-winning **The Spa** (daily 9am–9pm; tel: 04-959 2500), which offers treatments at the two sister luxury hotels in **Teluk Datai**. You can choose villas that blend beautifully with the rainforest at **The Datai**, or rooms with sweeping views of the gorgeous bay at **The Andaman**. If you are not sure what treatment to go for, try The Datai's signature massage, a combination of five techniques. The Spa's masseurs are all Balinese and were trained by luxury resort spa operator Mandara Spa. Afternoons are busy, so call ahead to book a slot.

Tanjung Rhu Beach

In the evening head to another northern beach, **Tanjung Rhu**, for the best sunset view in Langkawi. To get there, backtrack down Jalan Datai to Jalan Teluk Yu and turn left at the junction. Drive for about 12km (7½ miles) through more rural landscape until you hit Padang Lalang town.

Turn left at the roundabout to reach the **Four Seasons Resort** (tel: 04-950 8888). Spread over 19ha (48 acres), it is large even by the Four Seasons' standards, and has luxuriously spacious and exceptionally private rooms. The front portion is styled after the Alhambra gardens in Granada, Spain. The hotel also tries to make the most of its natural surroundings by employing a naturalist, the first in the history of this chain.

To catch the sunset, head beachside, either to the lounge, Rhu Bar or Ikan-Ikan restaurant. Then, cocktail in hand and weather permitting, watch a play of amazing hues as the sun disappears into the horizon. **Rhu Bar** has a busy Arabic decor and wonderful swings for curling up in and sipping sunset cocktails, which include some mean martinis. **Ikan-Ikan** has a more relaxed resort feel with a lovely open-air teak deck for lounging and a pavilion bar with cocktail seating. After the sunset, make your way to **Pantai Cenang** or **Kuah** for dinner.

Above: a restful corner at The Andaman
Right: get a soothing massage at The Datai

13. DIVING IN PULAU PAYAR *(see map, p48–49)*

Discover the rich and colourful underwater world at Langkawi's Pulau Payar Marine Park.

Take a speedboat or catamaran ride to Pulau Payar and spend the day there enjoying the marine ecosystem. This island package includes land and boat transfers, a picnic lunch and the RM5 environmental conservation charge. Boats depart from Kuah, but you can sometimes depart from Pantai Cenang. Just make sure your operator handles the permits needed for entering the marine park. Pack sunblock, drinking water and a dry T-shirt or towel in case it gets chilly on the boat ride back to Langkawi.

Pulau Payar Marine Park

Malaysia has some of the best coral reefs in the world, thanks to its shallow seas and plentiful sunlight. Some of this reef life can be experienced at **Pulau Payar Marine Park**, which has 36 different kinds of hard corals,

92 other marine invertebrates and 45 different kinds of fish. Consisting of four islands located about 19 nautical miles (30½ km) south of Kuah, the park's marine ecosystem can be discovered by snorkelling or scuba diving.

However, divers get a better deal for several reasons. Snorkellers are limited to the small house reef off Pulau Payar. Because the beach is tiny, it is reaching its capacity for snorkellers. What's more, some operators encourage feeding fish with bread. They also feed the black-tip reef sharks, which not only changes the sharks' diets but also causes them to be dependent on humans, and encourages them to come dangerously close to shore to feed.

Hence, the best way to enjoy Payar is to dive. If you have never dived before, this is a good opportunity to try a Discover Scuba Diving course, open to anyone aged 10 and above. The calm waters of Payar are ideal for beginners.

For certified divers, a dive package usually comprises two dives at the **Payar/Lembu/Kaca** island cluster. Diving here is easy and can be done year round, although during the rainy season (July to October), the seas can be rough and visibility low. Even on an average dive, visibility ranges from 5–15m (15–45ft), but the water is warm, ranging from 26–29°C (79–84°F).

Coral Gardens

One of the best dive sites is tiny – only 10sq m (108sq ft) in size. However, in ideal conditions, it is a spectacle of colour. Aptly named **Coral Gardens** after its many coloured soft corals, the site looks even prettier with shoals of fish swimming through. Look out for two special residents: a green moray

Above: Payar's clear, shallow waters are ideal for coral growth
Top right: a young snorkeller; **Bottom right:** divers *en route* to a dive spot

eel and a 1.2-m (4-ft)-long barracuda named Mustafa. Peering into crevices may reward you with the sight of cleaner shrimp and cowries. There are also three tyre reefs and a boat reef that are home to large groupers.

Lembu Rock and Pulau Kaca

Groupers and rock cods hang out at **Lembu Rock**. The main coral type here is hard coral. **Pulau Kaca** is interesting for its seven sunken fishing boats. Although the wooden wrecks are slowly disintegrating, they are still appealing for the large shoals of barracudas, snappers and black-tip reef sharks that are found here.

House Reef

The **House Reef** is home to a giant grouper named Toby who nuzzles up to divemasters he recognises. There are friendly rabbitfish here, and if you scour the rubble, you could spot mantis shrimp and moray eels. Boulder coral and barrel sponges are dominant.

Exploring Segantang Reef

Minimum numbers and good conditions are required for diving at **Pulau Segantang**, which is 10 minutes by boat from Payar. At **Segantang Reef**, there are barracudas, jacks, leopard sharks and, if you are really lucky, whale sharks. A plethora of anemones and their clownfish residents are a feature of **Segantang Rock**. Swim slowly to spot nudibranchs and murex shells.

When you hit the Payar beach for lunch, check out the Visitors' Centre, which has information on the park. There are also toilets and picnic tables on the beach, but no freshwater. Night dives can be arranged, but bear in mind that it takes one hour to get back to Langkawi.

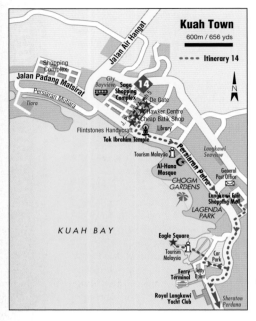

Kuah Town

600m / 656 yds

■■■■ Itinerary 14

Shopping Complex
Jalan Padang Matsirat
Persiaran Mutiara
Tiora
Jalan Air Hangat
City Bayview
Saga Shopping Complex
De Gate
Hawker Centre
Cheap Batik Shop
Library
Flintstones Handycraft
Tok Ibrahim Temple
Tourism Malaysia
Langkawi Seaview
Al-Hana Mosque
General Post Office
CHOGM GARDENS
Langkawi Fair Shopping Mall
LAGENDA PARK
KUAH BAY
Eagle Square
Tourism Malaysia
Car Park
Ferry Terminal
Jetty Point
Royal Langkawi Yacht Club
Sheraton Perdana
Persiaran Putra

14. Shopping in Kuah
(see map, p66)

Make the most of the duty-free status of this island with a shopping spree, and then end the day with a sunset cruise.

This shopping itinerary can occupy you for two hours or a whole afternoon. To catch the sunset cruise, be at the jetty by 5pm. You should book the cruise with Sunsail (www.sunsail.com; tel: 04-966 5869) at least two days in advance during the low season (June–Sept) and a week before during the rest of the year. The whole boat must be hired. The smallest vessel, for four passengers, costs RM750 (low season) for three hours, and comes with a skipper. You can tailor-make your itinerary, and snacks, beer and soft drinks are included.

Legend has it that the town of **Kuah** came about after a fight between two giants, Mat Cincang (of Machinchang Formation fame) and Mat Raya, at a wedding that resulted in pots and pans being thrown about and hot water and gravy being spilt. The gravy became the site of Kuah town, *kuah* being Malay for gravy; **Air Panas** is where the hot water splashed (there are actually hot springs here); and **Belanga Pecah** is where the broken pots were hurled.

Massive reclamation and the intense building in the 1990s have transformed Kuah from a fishing village into a tourist town promoting its duty-free status. Some character remains in a couple of rows of old shophouses on the main road, **Persiaran Putra**, between Jalan Air Hangat and Jalan Pandak Mayah 1. In contrast, the new buildings are characterless commercial spaces.

Start your shopping experience at the top end of **Jalan Pandak Mayah 5** at **Saga Shopping Centre**, a place where you can find household products, and then walk down the road towards Persiaran Putra. This road is lined with retailers selling artefacts from Malaysia and Asean countries. Shops include boutiques, wholesalers, wood specialists, and souvenir, handicraft and home decor outlets.

Tok Ibrahim Temple
When you are ready for a breather from your shopping, head down to Persiaran Putra, then turn left. Walk for about 100m (30ft) and you will come to a lane. Turn into this lane and you will come to a small Chinese temple. This is the **Tok Ibrahim temple**, which houses *datuk kong*, a deity in the form of a Chinese statue dressed in Muslim clothing, complete with two *keris* or Malay daggers. This fusion of Chinese and Islamic elements

is said to have started in Penang and is unique to the northern states of Peninsular Malaysia.

To the right of the temple is a gnarled fig tree, at the base of which there is an altar where there are different offerings, from joss sticks and flowers to the Malay staple rice dish, *nasi lemak*, and tobacco and betel nut. Fig trees are considered sacred by many cultures in Malaysia. Coming out of the temple, continue along the lane which curves back out to Persiaran Putra. Turn left, and you will see **Asia Restaurant** (daily 12–3pm, 6–10.30pm; tel: 04-966 6216), a good place for a late lunch.

Upmarket Shopping

If you are ready for more shopping, take a taxi to the **Langkawi Fair Shopping Complex**. This is the island's best mall and it hosts more upmarket retailers, such as the charming **Langkawi Arts Café**, a tiny art gallery with a cafe; **Ethnic Colours**, a jewellery store; and **Sunday Souvenirs**, which has knick knacks as well as home decor and furniture items.

Eagle Square

Next, take a taxi to **Eagle Square**, home to a massive statue of a Brahminy Kite. It is to this bird that a recent legend attributes the name of the island, with *lang* being short for *helang* or eagle, and *kawi* meaning reddish brown. More ancient texts name different origin sources, however (*see History & Culture*). Still, this island mascot is a nice tribute to the island's most common bird of prey, which lives and nests in mangrove areas, near estuaries and at fishing villages. The square is pleasant to stroll around in the evening.

Royal Langkawi Yacht Club

Go now to the **Royal Langkawi Yacht Club**, where you head out to sea on a yacht at dusk. Enjoy the breeze as your skipper travels through the straits along the southern coast of Langkawi and past islands like Pulau Ular, Pulau Singa and Pulau Kentut. The natural landscape here is dark grey rock, some of which contain pebbles of quartzite. This formation came about 270 to 300 million years ago during a period of cold, when the pebbles were 'dropped' by floating icebergs. Stop close to Awana Porto Malai jetty to watch the sun set over Pulau Tepor. Then return to shore to enjoy a dinner of steak or rack of lamb at **Charlie's Place** (8am–11pm; tel: 04-966 4078).

Top: the *datuk kong* greets you at the Tok Ibrahim temple
Left: the majestic Brahminy kite statue at Eagle Square

Leisure Activities

SHOPPING

Traditional craft souvenirs and artefacts are the draw of shopping in Penang and Langkawi, although neither offers the variety available in Kuala Lumpur.

Batik is plentiful, whether in the shape of *sarongs*, clothing, furnishing or artwork. For traditional *batik*, which is usually printed on cotton, you have a choice of local *batik*, which is made in the east coast states of Terengganu and Kelantan, or *batik* imported from Indonesia, which has different designs. Modern *batik* is locally produced and is usually printed on silk.

As for handicrafts and souvenirs, Malaysian products, such as pewter and indigenous basketry or weaving, make for nice gifts to take home. Otherwise, a lot of the handicraft is brought in from neighbouring countries like Indonesia, Thailand, Indochina and Burma. Some of it is designed or restored by Malaysian shop owners, but most is imported wholesale. Likewise, curio and antique collectors will enjoy browsing through pieces that have been sourced locally or from the rest of Asia.

Duty-free items, which are available everywhere and not only in duty-free shops, provide good bargains. Despite being zoned as duty-free, Langkawi does not have a particular advantage over Penang in terms of price. Things to look out for are electronics, watches, leather goods, cosmetics, sports equipment, gold coins, high-end fountain pens and musical instruments.

Resort apparel is also plentiful, affordable and well made. However, very large sizes can be rather difficult to find. During the major festivals of Chinese New Year, Hari Raya and Deepavali, the variety of ethnic or ethnic-inspired clothing and accessories improves, as does the availability of special festive foods.

Other than in malls where prices are fixed, it is best to shop around and bargain – particularly in places frequented by tourists. The best times to shop are during the annual nationwide six-week Mega Shopping Carnival starting in July, and at sales held by department stores throughout the year. Better bargains can be had if you pay cash (instead of by credit card) and, in Langkawi, by shopping during the low tourist season between July and September. At smaller shops, the first customer of the day usually gets the best price, because local shop owners believe it augurs well for business for the rest of the day.

PENANG

Ayer Itam
Bargain goods

The sidewalk stalls on the steps leading up to **Kek Lok Si** are good spots for buying cheap souvenirs, particularly Chinese or Buddhist items, such as incense sticks, old coins and windchimes. Cheap clothing, including souvenir T-shirts and caps, can also be a bargain here if shoppers are able to negotiate a low price.

Left: tourist browsing for souvenirs
Right: shoppers at a street market

Georgetown

Shops

Even non-shoppers will find delight in wandering through the capital's atmospheric old streets and viewing the shophouses. The most popular shopping stretches are along **Jalan Penang**, **Lebuh Chulia**, **Lebuh Campbell**, **Lebuh Kimberley** and **Jalan Burma**. Many shops sell modern-day goods, but in a few, the old, but unfortunately disappearing, trades are still found.

Interesting traditional buys include joss sticks, wooden clogs, bamboo blinds, traditional red lanterns and paper effigies. Local food products include biscuits and buns, freshly roasted local coffee and Penang's famous preserved nutmeg and mango. Local biscuits presented in rows of giant bottles come in a huge variety. Some must-tries include *tambun pneah* (mini biscuits with green bean and onion paste), *tau sar pneah* (pastry biscuits with a green bean filling), *hneah pneah* (sweet biscuits), sesame biscuits and pepper biscuits. Buns to try include *meeku* (traditional Chinese buns), baked *s*... *pau* (pork buns), any of the steamed *pa*... (buns), which have fillings such as *char s*... (barbecued pork), *tau sar* (red bean) and *li*... *yoong* (lotus seed).

One of the many Chinese teashops ca... provide a welcome respite as well as... chance to try some exotic tea. Porcelai... jewellery, coins, lamps, clocks and oth... *objet d'art* fill the antique shops, but onl... experts can be assured of walking away wi... genuine articles.

Leather luggage, accessories and shoe... jewellery, clothing and antiques are als... good buys. Beachwear like kaftans an... *sarongs* as well as traditional clothing suc... as Chinese *cheongsams*, the Malay *kebay*... for women or *baju Melayu* for men are th... among the best clothing buys.

Look out for specialist shops selling tra... ditional Nonya ladies' clothing and bead... shoes. Paired with *batik sarongs*, the blous... of this *pua teh*, or Nonya *kebaya*, is mad... of voile and has fine embroidered edges. Th... traditional clothing was well on its way t... obscurity until the Prime Minister's late wif... Datin Paduka Seri Endon Mahmood, reviv... it. Testament to its renewed popularity is i... availability in department stores. Howeve... for fine tailoring, seek out the speciali... shops. Beaded shoes are also unique loca... items. Commercial varieties are more com... mon and the beads tend to be larger and th... design coarser than on the handmade shoe...

Check out the Little India streets c... **Lebuh Pasar**, **Lebuh Queen**, **Lebuh Kin**... and **Lebuh China** for *saris*, fabric, gold jew... ellery, spices, decorative items and religiou... items like incense and statues of deities.

Markets

For a different shopping experience, chec... out the **Lorong Kulit Flea Market** (dail... 8am–2pm, unless it rains), which is not actu... ally on Lorong Kulit, but on Jalan Pera... behind the stadium. A mishmash of tras... and treasures, from Frank Sinatra 1940s h... singles to Beano comics, stilettos to hand... made silver bracelets, and fake Rolexes ar... laid out on tarpaulins. Watch amusin... medicine men hawk 'guaranteed' cures fo... everything from low libido to cancer. A not... of caution – be wary of things that look to...

Above: the Lebuh Campbell shopping stretch

slightly higher than in town, but good bargain-hunters will be happy with their finds. There is also an abundance of tailor shops here. Although it's no Saville Row, tailors here promptly make just about anything, with reasonable quality and for a sensible price. Tailor shops actually only take your measurements and then outsource the work to private tailors elsewhere; and some of these tailors work from home.

LANGKAWI

Kuah

Shops and Malls

The proclamation of Langkawi's duty-free status is apparent as soon as you land at the jetty with its giant signboard. Almost everything sold here is imported, so Langkawi lacks the quaint, locally-made goods of Georgetown. However, other than for the goods that are declared duty-free nationwide, prices are really better here. Certainly, this is where you will find the cheapest alcohol, cigarettes and chocolate in the country. Partake freely of the goodies while you are on the island, but note the limit on what you can take out of Langkawi, even if it's only to the mainland.

Locals come to Kuah to shop for household, personal items, particularly Indonesian *batik sarongs*, some electrical goods, as well as confectionary and seafood. Unfor-

ew to be second-hand, for while the market as attained official recognition, it still car-es its old taint of being a thieves' market. A sanitised version of this flea market can be experienced on Sundays from 1–8pm at rangin Mall next to KOMTAR.

Another local shopping experience is the *asar malam* or **night markets**, which are usually set up from around 6pm. These markets at held in a different location nightly o check with your hotel or Tourism Malaysia for the latest schedules. Mingle with the locals as they haggle over fresh produce, cheap clothing and household goods.

Malls

Penang's malls do not offer the volume or variety of Kuala Lumpur, but good bargains can be picked up during sales periods and the air-conditioning beats the mid-day heat outside. Popular malls are **Prangin Mall** on Jalan Dr Lim Chwee Leong, next to KOM-TAR; the classy **Plaza Gurney** on Gurney Drive, which carries many international labels; and **One Stop** in Midlands Park, Jalan Burma, which has lower-end retail outlets.

Batu Ferringhi

Shops and Markets

Here in this short stretch, you get the gamut of *batik*, souvenirs, antiques and handicraft (*see Itinerary 3*). Quality artwork and Asian artefacts can be found at **Yahong Art Gallery**. There is also a **night market** for tourists. Prices here would probably be

Above: interior of the popular Prangin Mall in Penang
Right: Batu Ferringhi night market

tunately, there isn't a wide range. The larger shops are **Teow Soon Huat Supermarket** on the fringe of town, **Saga Shopping Centre** on Jalan Pandak Mayah 5, **Samudra Duty Free Department Store** in the Langkawi Fair Shopping Centre, and the **Jetty Point Duty Free Complex** where the ferries arrive and depart. Note that the smaller mom-and-pop shops can sometimes offer even better deals.

Tourist shops tout a variety of souvenir and household items made of bamboo, lacquer, wood, stone, ceramics or glass from all over Southeast Asia. The only goods that might be considered Malaysian are indigenous crafts from Sabah and Sarawak. Souvenir shops line **Jalan Pandak Mayah 5** and are housed in the huge **Langkawi Fair Shopping Complex** (*see Itinerary 14*).

Outskirts and Langkawi Airport

You can buy *batik* at the **Atma Alam Batik Art Village** in Padang Matsirat and quality Asian art and crafts at **SunVillage** and also **Sunmall**, which are located across from each other in Pantai Tengah. There is a small, fancy shopping arcade at the **Four Seasons Resort** in Tanjung Rhu, with exclusive brands and an art gallery featuring Asian works curated by the renowned Kuala Lumpur-based Galeri Taksu. The **Langkawi International Airport** has a decent selection of goodies for last-minute shoppers.

EATING OUT

Penang is a food paradise, with an amazing range of tastes that are drawn from its multi-ethnic heritage. The best-known food is Chinese hawker food, found in the coffeeshops or hawker centres that pepper the island. These informal eateries are usually open all day, although some are open only at night. A large variety of fare can be sampled at the popular **Gurney Drive**, but below is a list of culinary chart-toppers.

Originally from Penang (but now found throughout the country) are two cuisines: Nonya and *nasi kandar*. The former is the food of Straits Chinese, which is infused with Malay spices. Penang Nonya food is, moreover, influenced by neighbouring Thailand, and so favours a sour, tangy flavour. Many restaurants purport to dish up nonya food, but good eateries are hard to come by, as the best dishes are still home cooked.

Nasi kandar was literally lugged around on a long pole (*kandar*) and is the food of the Indian Muslims. A meal consists of rice and curried meats and seafood. Recently, *nas*

Above: *batik* art for sale
Right: cuttlefish at a cuttlefish and spinach hawker stall

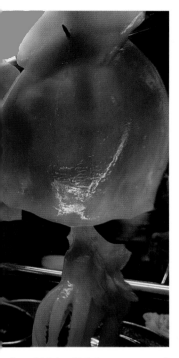

ndar, which is widely known as *mamak* od, has become so popular that *nasi kan-r* chains have mushroomed. However, the thenticity of the food at many of these aces is questionable.

Malay, Thai, Indian and Chinese cuisines e easily found, as is international fare. verything, from generic 'Western meal' eaks and fish and chips, to Japanese, orean and Italian, is served. American fast od and coffeehouse chains are ubiquitous.

Langkawi, in contrast, has little indige- us fare other than Malay food, which the trepid might want to try at the night mar- t or roadside stalls in villages. Kuah has od and cheap Chinese and Thai seafood staurants. Otherwise, hotel restaurants fer the gamut of local and Western meals.

In the recommendations below, price cate- ries for a meal for two consisting of a cal rice meal with three dishes, or a three- urse Western meal, without drinks, are ted as follows:

$ = under RM30

$$ = RM30–60

$$$ = RM60 and above

PENANG

Laksa, the best-known hawker fare in Penang, comprises steamed rice vermicelli in a fish-based, sour and very spicy soup. The best *laksa* is found in the **Ayer Itam Market** and **Balik Pulau market**.

If it's a milder experience you're seek- ing, try *char koay teow* (fried flat noodles with prawns, cockles and egg). Favourite outlets are **Sisters** at Jalan Macalister (near the junction with Jalan Perak) in the morn- ing, and a stall near a coffeeshop in **Lorong Selamat** in the afternoon.

If you like spicy dishes, sample the curry *mee* in **Bee Hooi Coffeeshop** in Pulau Tikus in the morning. The shop is at the junction of Jalan Burma and Lorong Pulau Tikus. Another version of a spicy noodle dish is *Hokkien mee*, a prawn-based soup; the best example is found in the coffeeshop at the **junction of Jalan Burmah and Jalan Cantonment** in the morning.

For non-spicy soup-based noodles, try the *koay teow th'ng* at **Hai Oan Coffeeshop**, located on Jalan Burma near the junction with Lorong Macalister; this dish is avail- able only in the morning and usually sells out before noon. The Hainanese Chicken Rice at **Fatty Loh**, near Tanjung Bungah, oppo- site the Chinese Swimming Club, is also worth seeking out.

For sweet desserts, the best *cendol* (green bean strands in shaved ice and coconut milk) and *ais kacang* (shaved ice with grass jelly, red beans and sweet corn) can be sampled at the **Teochew Chendul stall** at the junc- tion of Jalan Penang and Lebuh Keng Kwee, next to Joo Hooi Café.

Georgetown

Edelweiss Café
38 Armenian Street
Tel: 04-261 8935
Set in a beautiful 1890s Chinese shophouse, this café is a hangout for local artists and conservationists. Grab a table in the airwell and cool down with a nutmeg juice. The menu is diverse, and includes sandwiches, salads, macaroni and cheese, and local dishes like fried rice and Malay *mee soto*. Afford- able three-course set lunch menus and bot- tled beer available. **$$**

Kapitan's
93 Lebuh Chulia
Tel: 04-264 1191
Open around the clock, this eatery serves up Northern Indian fare. The soft, fresh *naan* bread and sweet or mint chutneys best accompany the mild tandoori chicken, marinated in the restaurant's signature spice mix and cooked in ovens imported from India. An iced fruit *lassi* (yoghurt drink) is the perfect complement to the spicy food. **$**

Nonya Baba Cuisine
44 Nagore Road
Tel: 04-227 8035
Formerly called Dragon King, the restaurant in this restored shophouse serves what is probably the best *Nonya* food in town. Must-try dishes are *chun piah* (spring rolls), *kerabu moknee* (fungus salad), *kari kapitan* (chicken curry), and sea coconut dessert. **$$**

Shang Palace
Level 2, Shangri-la Hotel, Magazine Road
Tel: 04-262 2622
Offering fine dining in a plush environment, this Cantonese restaurant's specialties include suckling pig (pre-order only), homemade *tofu* and steamed tiger garoupa. The lunchtime Hong Kong *dim sum* is popular. On Monday and Thursday nights, the buffet features oyster, salmon and *sashimi*. **$$$**

Shusi Banana Leaf Restaurant
71 Penang Street
A no-frills outfit in the heart of Little India that dishes up typical South Indian fare. Indulge in homemade breads including *thosai* and *puri*. The mutton curry is excellent. Order a hot *teh tarik* ('pulled' tea) for a filling, frothy beverage. **$**

Tajuddin Hussain
49 & 51 Queen Street
Tel: 04-262 5367
Having been around for 45 years, Tajuddin Hussain has perfected its *nasi kandar*. The huge dining area is simply furnished, with wooden tables and plastic chairs. While the outlet specialises in tomato rice and roast chicken, the *nasi briyani* is also worth trying. Friday-only specials consist of goose and turkey in a curry. **$**

Ayer Itam

Kek Lok Si Vegetarian Restaurant
Kek Lok Si
Tel: 04-828 8142
This Chinese vegetarian restaurant has be in operation for 14 years. The menu is exte sive and specialties include roasted mo chicken in Szechuan spicy sauce, a Thai *t yam* soup, *tofu* dishes and noodle soup Alternatively, order a set meal (rice with se eral dishes) or try a steamboat (a hotp where you cook your own food). Alcoh is not served. **$$**

Batu Ferringhi

The Bungalow
Lone Pine Hotel
Tel: 04-881 1511
Facing the hotel pool and the casuarina-lin beach, this restaurant housed in a coloni building has a truly tropical location wi indoor and outdoor seating. At night, t atmosphere is very romantic. The menu co centrates on Hainanese dishes, but includ dishes such as fish curry, chicken rice ar *filet mignon*. **$$$**

Mario's Restaurant
152-B Batu Ferringhi
Tel: 04-881 3775
Wood-fired pizza, grilled salmon, pasta ar a supreme cappuccino are highlights on t menu at this authentic Italian restaurar Located opposite the Golden Sands Hotel. has a breezy café feel by day and a war fine-dining atmosphere at night. Breakfast also served at this restaurant. The bar serv a good selection of Italian, Chilean and Au tralian wines. **$$$**

Kampung Restaurant
411 Batu Ferringhi
A family-run concern opposite Lone Pir Hotel with tables and chairs, set out on t grounds of a Malay village house. By nigl fairy lights and oil lamps make the plac very pretty. Breakfasts here are good, as a the Malaysian dishes, including spic Eurasian devil curry, Malay *ayam mas lemak* (chicken curry) and beef *rendar (beef stew), and Thai green curry. Carlsbe and Thai Chang beer available. **$**

Gigi's By the Sea
Shangri-la's Golden Sands Resort
Tel: 04-886 1911
Bright Mediterranean colours echo the delightful menu at this award-winning bistro. Using imported ingredients, signature dishes include Moroccan roasted lamb rack, lamb shank stew, a seafood combination called Fishing Bird, and an excellent Greek salad. Weekends host barbecues and every night sees a Latin band. The wine list centres on Australian vintages. **$$$**

LANGKAWI

Kuah

Asia Restaurant
4A & 4A Persiaran Putra
Tel: 04-966 6216
'We serve good food', this restaurant declares on its business card, and it's no lie. Hearty home-cooked vegetarian dishes include fried rice, steamed oyster mushrooms and *sambal tofu*. This unpretentious 1970s-style Chinese restaurant outlet is part of the Langkawi family-owned Asia Hotel. Chinese-style seafood is also on the menu. **$**

Charlie's Place
Langkawi Yacht Club
Tel: 04-966 4078
New Zealand steaks and rack-of-lamb in Jack Daniels sauce as well as a hearty seafood platter are the specialties of this restaurant, which overlooks the marina. Checked tablecloths and friendly staff add to its appeal. Local goodies include a decent Malay set platter and a sumptuous seafood platter. Arrive early for dinner and enjoy a beer while watching the sunset. **$$$**

ern Thai
201–202 Pusat Dagangan Kelamas
Jalan Mutiara 2
Tel: 019-493 6862
A Thai cook heads the kitchen at this established local restaurant, where diners select their seafood from a display. The menu offers an assortment of Southeast Asian delights, including steamed fish in a tasty, soupy sauce, spicy *kerabu* salad, and Chinese-style butter prawns. **$**

right: view from Charlie's Place

Wonderland
Jalan Mutiara 2
Tel: 012-494 6555
This no-frills eatery is popular with locals for its good-value Cantonese food. Recommendations include home-style *tofu*, a variety of fresh greens stir-fried with garlic, *kung pao* chicken or squid stir-fried with dried chilli, and shrimp in batter cooked in a spicy tamarind sauce. **$**

Pantai Cenang/Pantai Tengah

Beach Garden Resort Bistro/Beergarden
Pantai Cenang
Tel: 04-955 1363
The best margaritas in Langkawi are at this German-run beachside eatery. Tables are on the sand and offer views of the sunset. The bistro serves tasty pizzas, pastas, salads and grilled seafood. During the day, shade-lovers can opt for the covered dining pavilion. **$$**

Bon Ton Restaurant and Resort
Pantai Cenang
Tel: 04-955 6787
An innovative Asian-spiced menu includes eclectic starters like pita bread with parmesan and harissa. Main dishes of beef and lamb are tender and juicy, and the side salads suitably interesting. After dinner, tour the antique Malay houses that make up the resort. Diners should arrive early for *tapas* (from 5pm) and a sunset view. **$$$**

Matahari Malay Restaurant
Sunvillage, Jalan Teluk Baru, Pantai Tengah
Tel: 04-955 6200
A charming Balinese-influenced ambience weaves its magic at this Malay restaurant. Meals are as good as homemade as they are prepared by cooks from the local village. Sit cross-legged in a cabana or dine by a landscaped pond, and feast on village-style *nasi campur*, a platter of 11 dishes including *satay*, local *rendang tok* and curry chicken. Dinner is served from 6–11pm. $$$

Red Tomato Splash Beach Café
Pantai Cenang
Tel: 04-4955 3088
Great breakfasts and superb Lavazza coffee are served here. The restaurant is pork-free, and a variety of breads is served, including fresh crusty rolls and bruschetta, eggs and pancakes. Delicious drinks include herbal teas and fresh fruit juices. The beachside café is bright and cheerful, and jazz music plays on the stereo. In keeping with the laid-back feeling, breakfast is served until 2pm. $$

Sun Café
Shop No 8, Sunmall
Jalan Teluk Baru, Pantai Tengah
Tel: 04-955 8300
Sun Café's carefully prepared meals come at really reasonable prices, belying the classy European look of this breezy café. The food is prepared with organic ingredients, and the menu has a perfect assortment of hearty sandwiches, thin-crust pizzas, vegetarian meals and spicy local fare. The *creme brulee* and milkshakes are delightful. If for nothing else, it is worth visiting just to check out the fancy toilets. $$

Elsewhere

Mare Blue
B5–6 Perdana Quay
Telaga Harbour Park, Pantai Kok
Tel: 04-959 3830
Lobster with linguine, imported beef tenderloin and tiramisu make up a wonderful Italian meal at this cosy restaurant. The pizzas here are popular. Sit inside on comfy sofas or outside for *al fresco* dining. $$$

Restoran Siti Fatimah
Jalan Kampung Tok Senik (near the hospital)
Tel: 04-955 2754
The huge buffet spread of typical Malay *kampung* or village fare includes a large selection of *kerabu* or salads, usually eaten with a spicy *sambal* dip, *ikan bakar* (grilled fish), and a range of curries and *rendang* (stew). No alcohol is served. Buffet from 7am–5pm; *a la carte* till 11pm. $

Shrimpz Restaurant
Prawn Farm, Jalan Bukit Malut (near the Langkawi Golf Club)
Tel: 04-966 3211
As its name suggests, tiger prawns are the draw here. Try them in black pepper, in Thai *tom yam* spicy soup, barbecued or simply steamed. The menu also includes Chinese dishes and *mee gulung*, a Langkawi noodle dish that is almost obsolete. Private cabanas suggest a Balinese influence. $$

Above: garden in Matahari Malay Restaurant; **Left**: the Sun Café

NIGHTLIFE

In **Penang**, the Upper Penang Road area is home to the trendiest nightlife on the island. Music from live bands and DJs resonates from **clubs**, **pubs** and **eateries** housed in carefully restored heritage buildings. The **Garage**, with its variety of nightspots, is the most popular place. Conveniently, local food stalls are just an amble away for post-dancing supper or late-night cup of hot *teh tarik*.

Live bands also play in **hotel lounges** in town and in the hotels in Batu Ferringhi. Oldies, current hits and audience requests are *de rigueur*. Most of the acts are talented Filipino imports and most are indistinguishable from each other.

Karaoke is very popular among locals, and some of the karaoke bars are upmarket and provide the stage for making big business deals. Song lists are impressive, from evergreens to last week's chart-toppers. In most places, private rooms are available, as are snacks and alcohol. Many hotels have karaoke lounges, but two in town to check out are the **Song Bird** in One Stop Midland and **Redbox** in Plaza Gurney.

However, the phenomenon of **supper** is probably the most entrenched after-dark activity. Families, couples and buddies come out late, particularly on weekends, and gather at Chinese hawker centres and *mamak* (Indian) stalls until the wee hours of the morning. Football has an almost cult following in Malaysia, and *mamak* stalls, in particular, attract hordes of fans with huge television screens playing live matches.

The trendy and the young gravitate towards air-conditioned and Internet-wired **American coffeehouse chains** such as Starbucks, **Taiwanese bubble teahouses**, and local variations thereof. These establishments stay open till 1am on weekends.

Alcohol in Malaysia is heavily taxed and, therefore, expensive. However, drink promotions are frequently held and happy hours lower the cost of a night out. Most places sell local beers and hard liquor, although you can just as easily get imported stuff, and wine has also become popular. If you are clubbing, note that Penangites do not dress up much, but having said that, slippers and shorts are not acceptable attire.

Most bars and restaurants in **Langkawi** offer a good range of imported beers, liquor and wines that you cannot get on the mainland. However, despite the relatively low price of alcohol here, the island has a sleepy nightlife. Things get very quiet after 10pm and nightspots generally close by 1am. Some hotel lounges have live music, and there are a few pubs. The best way to enjoy Langkawi by night is to take a peaceful walk on the beach and listen to the gentle surf, or even better, lay a *sarong* on the sand and sip wine while watching the stars. Some hotels offer natural nocturnal excitement with jungle treks (*See Sports*).

PENANG

Pubs & Bars

20 Leith St
20 Lebuh Leith
Tel: 04-261 8573
Formerly part of the Cheong Fatt Tze Mansion that sits just opposite, this laid-back wine bar and Japanese bistro exudes old-world charm in an antique setting. The ornate bar is decorated with gilded Chinese bridal

Right: 20 Leith Street bar

bed carvings. Imbibe inside or outside, or shoot pool while enjoying funky CD music or even the occasional live band.

Chic!
403 Burma Road, Pulau Tikus
Tel: 04-226 2328
A sophisticated new two-storey outlet, Chic! claims to have Penang's largest cocktail menu and serves premium liquors, wines and champagnes. Downstairs is a bar and café with free Internet access. Upstairs is a dance space where serious house music is spun.

Cubar Club
75 Gurney Drive
Tel: 04-227 9823
This popular multiple-outlet nightspot comprises a wine and cigar bar on the ground floor, a lounge on the first floor, a barbecue pork rib restaurant on the second floor, and karaoke rooms at the top. Its selling point is a beer garden with wooden decks and fairylights, and here you can sip Italian wine and enjoy a *Romeo y Julieta*, or shoot some pool. Open daily 5pm–3am.

Hong Kong Bar
371 Lebuh Chulia
Tel: 04-261 9796
Opened in 1920, this institution was a regular hangout for military personnel based in Butterworth. Today, it still attracts an assortment of prominent characters, many of whose photographs, medals and plaques plaster the walls and whose stories fill the guest book. The chatty owners have a knack for remembering faces and names.

Shamrock Irish Pub
Ground floor, MWE Plaza, Farquhar Street
Tel: 04-264 4748
This history-filled corner of Penang is home to an Irish pub, although here the traditional cosy pub feel is sacrificed for a more open, breezy feel and tables spill outdoors onto the pavement. The regulars can be very welcoming. Thursday is ladies' night.

Slippery Senoritas
The Garage
Tel: 04-263 6868
A salsa club and Mexican restaurant, the DJ spin a combination of R&B, house and current hits until 10pm when a live band take over. Bands change every three months. It cocktail menu offers 69 variations, which bartenders will deliver to you with an impressive stunt or two *a la* 'flair' bartending, for which they are the northern champs. Ladies' night on Wednesday.

Soho Free House Pub
50 Jalan Penang
Tel: 04-263 3331
A British tavern with a pool table, football on the telly, and hearty pub grub, this tiny place draws local professionals as well as Britons and Australians. Make the most of happy hours from 5–9pm, as the regular crowd does, when beer is a steal at RM5.50. Guinness on tap is RM14 a pint.

Dance Clubs
ChillOut Club
The Gurney, Gurney Drive
Tel: 04-370 7000
This club is actually a complex of four bars and clubs. Each club plays a different style of music, including funk and R&B. One out

---

Above: Cubar has a great beer garden and good sea views from the upper floors

...et is a wine terrace. The place is packed on weekends and on Wednesdays, when it is ladies' night. Post-partying, chill out at any of the cafés or 24-hour local eating outlets right on the doorstep of the complex.

GloPenang and **Lush**
The Garage
Tel: 04-261 1066
These sister clubs play trance and house music. Every Wednesday and Friday, Glo hosts a live dance show with themes ranging from acrobatics to Arabian nights. Lush, the newer club, has a long happy hour – all night long – on Sundays and Mondays, and from 5–10pm during the rest of the week. The cover charge at either club is RM25 and the fare is inclusive of one drink. Wednesday is ladies' night.

Lounges

Revolving Restaurant
City Bayview Hotel, 25A Lebuh Farquhar
Tel: 04-263 3161
Open until midnight, this is a place you could easily spend all night enjoying the good-value sunset buffet dinner. Alternatively, as night falls, watch upper Georgetown light up over a drink or an ice cream dessert. A band plays every evening.

Arts & Culture

In the spirit of the hotel's heyday, the Eastern & Oriental Hotel hosts dinner and **ballroom dancing** on Thursdays between 9.30pm and midnight. The band plays music from the 1940s and 1960s. Non-diners are also welcome to the dance floor, but a cover charge applies.

    Traditional Chinese opera is a dying art, but it is still performed in temples during major festivals and on the birthdays of key deities. A good place to see this disappearing art form is at the Kuan Yin Teng during the 'three enlightenment days of Kuan Yin', which fall on the 19th day of the second, sixth and ninth lunar month.

    Regular **theatre** productions are staged by The **Actors Studio Greenhall** (www.the actorsstudio.com.my), which is located near the E&O Hotel. Check media for other productions, and look out in particular for the annual Penang-YTL Arts Festival.

Right: traditional Chinese opera singer

LANGKAWI

Kuah

For live music, head to **Some Place Else** at the Sheraton Perdana Resort, which also has a small dance floor.

Pantai Cenang/Pantai Tengah

Enjoy cocktails or wine from an extensive wine list at Bon Ton Restaurant and Resort's **Chin Chin Bar**, housed in a restored antique Chinese shophouse. The airy and expansive lobby lounge of the **Pelangi Beach Resort** hosts live bands. For a cosy ambience, visit its lush and candlelit **Champor-Champor** bar, or sip margaritas under the stars at the **Beach Garden Resort Bistro**. End the night with a superb dessert and coffee at the **Sun Café** on Pantai Tengah.

Pantai Kok

Groove to more live music at **Mutiara Burau Bay Beach Resort**'s cheerful **Sea Shell Beach Café**. You can also select wine from the large walk-in wine cellar next door, the **Bayside Cellars**. For something quieter, check out **Sampan Bar** (happy hours 6–7.30pm), also in the resort.

CALENDAR OF EVENTS

Festivals are a great reason to be in **Penang**, as these are occasions at which local colour and vibrant traditions transform the island like at no other time of the year. A tradition that cuts across ethnicity is the 'open house', when people visit celebrants to wish them well and feast on special holiday goodies. In **Langkawi**, celebrations are more muted except for Muslim festivals. Look up the Tourism Malaysia website (www.tourism. gov.my) for a full list of events.

The Muslim calendar marks two big festivals. **Hari Raya Puasa** is a celebration of the first day of the Muslim month of Shawal, following a month of strict fasting and prayers during Ramadan. Muslims usher in Hari Raya Puasa by attending prayers at the mosque, followed by visiting and the holding of 'open house'. Check out the Pasar Ramadan, markets that are held only during the month before Raya, where special goodies and food is sold.

Hari Raya Haji is when Muslims mark the end of the annual pilgrimage in Mecca. There are special early morning prayers and sermons at mosques throughout the country. Buffaloes, goats and sheep are sacrificed and the meat distributed to the poor and needy. In Langkawi, the atmosphere around mosques at about 10am is particularly festive.

Chinese New Year falls in late January or early February. This 15-day celebration by the Chinese begins on the eve of the Lunar New Year, when family members get together over a sumptuous reunion dinner. Family gatherings, prayers, holding 'open house', lion dances, and eating, particularly of *yee sang*, a fish salad, are the order of the day throughout the festival. For Hokkiens, the ninth day is significant for those praying to the Kitchen God. The last day, *Chap Goh Mei*, is regarded as a night of courtship and is celebrated on Gurney Drive in Penang and at Dataran Lang in Langkawi.

Among the non-festival events bookended by festivals is **Colours of Malaysia** (May/June), a month of exhibitions of Malaysia's culture and craft and food promotions. The countdown to **Hari Kebangsaan (National Day)** (31 Aug), a celebration of Malaysia's independence from British

rule, is a boisterous event in Penang, held annually at the Esplanade. The **Mega Shopping Carnival** (July/August) is a six-week-long nationwide sale.

Deepavali (October/November) or the Festival of Lights is a major Hindu festival, a celebration of good over evil. Different ethnic groups link it to different deities, including Lakshmi and Vishnu, Rama, Krishna and Kali. A purifying oil bath is taken early in the morning and rows of oil lamps lit. After praying at the temple, the merry-making and eating begin. November is also the month that sees sailboats aplenty in Penang and Langkawi during the **Raja Muda International Regatta**.

Christmas (December 25) is celebrated by Christians with church masses, carolling, shopping, gift exchange and 'open house'.

PENANG

January/February

Chingay Parade: First held in 1880 to honour the five deities serving as patrons of different Chinese dialect groups, the *chingay* parade has become a fun event held at the Padang during Chinese New Year, when troupes show off their skills in balancing giant flags on 6–12m (20–40 ft) tall poles on various parts of their body.

Thaipusam (late January/early February): One of the most visually spectacular Hindu festivals celebrated in Penang, it commemorates Lord Muruga or Subramaniam, the deity representing virtue and bravery. On the festival's eve, a silver chariot carries the image of the deity from the Chettiar Temple in Penang Street to the hilltop Sri

Above: a *kavadi* bearer at Thaipusam

Arulmigu Balathandayuthapani Temple in Waterfall Road. Devotees follow, or line the streets, smashing coconuts and making offerings. On Thaipusam day, up to 600,000 bearers of *kavadi* (a wooden frame to carry milk and offerings) and milk pots go up to the temple, some pierced with skewers and hooks as penance, many enveloped in the warmth of family and friends.

April/May/June

Songkran (mid-April): At the Thai and Burmese temples in Lorong Burma, Songkran (the beginning of the new solar year) is celebrated with enthusiasm and much water, which is believed to wash away bad luck. After a bathing rite for the statue of Buddha and the monks, celebrants joyfully splash each other and anyone else in the vicinity, including the unwary tourist.

Wesak Day (early May): The most significant festival for Buddhists commemorates the birth, enlightenment and death of Buddha. Temples are packed with devotees offering prayers and giving alms.

International Dragon Boat Festival: Coinciding with *Bak Chang* or Chinese rice dumpling festival, this colourful race (www.penangdragonboat.com) sees teams of 12 to 20 paddlers rowing furiously for 800m (¼ mile) or 1km (½ mile) to the beat of drums, in traditional Chinese boats decorated with dragonheads. The festival is held at the Teluk Bahang dam.

July/August/September

Hungry Ghost Festival (end-August): The Chinese believe that during this seventh month of the lunar calendar, the gates of hell open and souls in purgatory wander the earth, and must be appeased with food offerings. Roadsides will be lined with little altars and burning candles and 'hell money'. During this time, you may be able to catch rare Chinese opera performances in the back lanes.

Mooncake or Lantern Festival (August/September): The Chinese Mooncake Festival on the fifteenth day of the eighth lunar month celebrates the overthrow of the Mongols in China through the use of cakes to smuggle messages. Today, the festival is celebrated with colourful lanterns and the mooncake's (message-less) fillings have become

quite varied, although the traditional red bean or lotus seed paste are still popular.

LANGKAWI

January/February

Le Tour de Langkawi: This 10-stage international race (www.tdl.com.my) attracts some of the world's top cyclists. Starting in Langkawi, cyclists traverse the length of Peninsular Malaysia before finishing in Kuala Lumpur.

Langkawi Ironman Triathlon: The elite of triathlon racing participate in this competition (www.ironmanlangkawi.com.my). The race includes a swim off the waters of Kuah, a cycle around Langkawi and a marathon run, ending at Dataran Lang. Winners qualify for the Ironman Triathlon World Championships in Hawaii in October.

March

BMW Royal Langkawi International Regatta: Yachters and spectators enjoy a week of competition and fun at this regatta (www.langkawiregatta.com) hosted at the Royal Langkawi Yacht Club.

December

Langkawi International Maritime & Aerospace Exhibition (LIMA) (December): This biennial exhibition (www.lima.com.my) draws big crowds. The Asia-Pacific's biggest exhibition showcases the latest, state-of-the-art equipment and technology in the aerospace, air defence, maritime and civil industries. Held at the Mahsuri International Exhibition Centre, the most popular event are the appearances by aerobatic teams.

Right: giant joss sticks during the Hungry Ghost month

Practical
Information

GETTING THERE

enang

y Air

enang is linked by air directly to the
Malaysian capital, Kuala Lumpur, Langkawi
and Johor Bahru, as well as to Singapore,
angkok, Nagoya, Medan, Xiamen, and
Madras. Kuala Lumpur is an hour's flight
way, and **Malaysia Airlines** (24-hour call
entre tel: 03-7846 3000; 1-300-883 000
ithin Malaysia; www.malaysiaairlines.com)
es there from over 100 destinations. Check
ut their online offers, and half-price domes-
c fares (limited seats) and night tourist fares.
Penang, the office is in KOMTAR.

Likewise, local budget airlines **AirAsia**
www.airasia.com) offers extremely cheap
nline fares. Other popular airlines are
ingapore Airlines (tel: 04-226 3201), **Thai
irways International** (tel: 04-226 6000),
nd **Cathay Pacific** (tel: 04-226 0411).

The **Penang International Airport** (tel:
4-643 4411) is in Bayan Lepas, about 20km
2½ miles) to Georgetown and 32km (20
iles) to Batu Ferringhi. Taxis from the air-
ort booth use coupons (tel: 012-417 9540).
ride to Georgetown is RM35, and to Batu
erringhi, RM50. A bus also goes hourly to
engkalan Weld in Georgetown (6am–
Opm). Many hotels do pick-ups. Car hire
also available at the airport.

y Rail

he National Railways, **KTMB** (tel: 03-2267
200 Kuala Lumpur; www.ktmb.com.my),
erates services to Butterworth on the main-
nd from Singapore and from the Thai bor-
er, where you can connect from Bangkok.
he journey from Kuala Lumpur takes nine
ours. The trains are modern and the ser-
ce efficient. Express services make mini-
al stops, are air-conditioned, and have
uffet cars serving simple meals. The fare
arts at RM30 for second-class seats on the
ght services. There are also sleeping berths

on the night services, with compartments
for two and dormitories. You can reserve
tickets online. In Butterworth, the railway
station is beside the ferry terminal.

By Road

Penang is linked by road via the 13½-km
(8½-mile) Penang Bridge to the north and
south of the Peninsula on the North-South
Highway. From the north, Penang is over
an hour's drive from Bukit Kayu Hitam at
the Thai border, and from the south, it is
five hours from Kuala Lumpur and another
four hours from Johor Bahru and Singapore.
If you are driving, have change available
for tolls (about RM40 from Kuala Lumpur
to Penang) and note where the petrol stations are (for a highway map, go to
www.plus.com.my/map_overview.asp). You
pay toll fees for the bridge only when entering the island from the mainland.

Long-distance express buses go to Penang
from anywhere in the country, as well as
from Thailand (Bangkok, Haadyai and
Phuket) and Singapore (via Kuala Lumpur).
From Kuala Lumpur, there are departures
hourly from 7.30–12.30am and fares are
under RM30 one-way. All buses are air-conditioned and have toilets; there are also exec-
utive or VIP coaches with more legroom.

Recommended companies are **Plusliner/
Nice** (tel: 03-2272 1586; www.plusliner.
com), which stops in Georgetown; **Gunung**

eft: Penang Bridge is one of the longest bridges in Southeast Asia
ight: Air Asia offers budget flights to Penang and Langkawi

Raya (tel: 04-660 2100); and **Sri Maju Sarata/Aneka Jasaramai** (tel: 03-2070 1279; www.srimaju.com). Buses must stop at the **Sungai Nibong Express Bus Terminal** near Penang Bridge, 30 minutes from Georgetown. For a nominal fee, most companies will shuttle you to town (KOMTAR) where they have an office; otherwise catch a bus (25, 66 and 69) or a taxi (about RM15). Be warned that the air-conditioning on buses can be extremely cold, so take a jacket with you, especially if you are travelling at night. Buses sometimes make a half-hour pit stop along the highway.

From Thailand, minivans travel in the morning and early afternoon daily to Penang from Haadyai (4 hours), Phuket (12 hours) and even Bangkok (20 hours). Fares range from RM20 to RM75.

There are also taxis from all major towns, but these are expensive and some will insist on waiting until the taxi is full (four passengers) before moving. The taxi stands are usually near the bus terminals. Go early in the morning. Note that if your transport stops in Butterworth on the mainland, you can just hop onto the ferry *(see By Sea below)*.

By Sea
Before Penang Bridge was built, ferries were the only way to get to the island from Butterworth. Those services still operate (5.30–11pm) and make for an enjoyable 20-minute ride. Cars are charged the same fare as going on the bridge; passengers pay about RM1. In Penang, the dock is at Pengkalan Weld, where there are plenty of taxis and buses, including a free tourist shuttle bus that goes around Georgetown.

There are also daily ferries from Langkawi to Penang at 2.30pm (via Pulau Payar) and 5.30pm (tel: 04-264 3088, 016-443 3993). The journey takes two hours and costs RM40 one way. Ferries from Medan, Indonesia depart at 10.30am and 11am daily except Sunday when there is only one service at 10.30am. The fare is RM90. Call **Fast Ferry Ventures** (tel: 04-262 0802).

Cruise ships also call on Penang and Langkawi from Singapore and Port Klang (near Kuala Lumpur), and some go on to Phuket. Call **Star Cruises** (tel: 03-309 2828; www.starcruises.com).

Langkawi
By Air
You can get to Langkawi by direct flig[ht] from Kuala Lumpur, Singapore and Londo[n]. The most frequent flights are on **Malaysi[a] Airlines** (tel: 03-7846 3000; www.malays[ia]airlines.com). Cheap fares are available o[n] **AirAsia** (www.airasia.com). **SilkAir** (tel: 6[3] 6223 8888) flies regularly from Singapore.

The **Langkawi International Airport** [at] Padang Mat Sirat is 20km (12½ miles) [to] Kuah, 8km (5 miles) to Pantai Cenang an[d] 43km (26½ miles) to Teluk Datai. Taxis us[e] a coupon system but all hotels will pick gues[ts] up. There are car rental agencies at the airpor[t].

By Rail
See rail information in the Penang sectio[n] on page 88. The difference is that you di[s]embark at Arau to get to Kuala Perlis an[d] Alor Setar to get to Kuala Kedah. The jou[r]ney from Kuala Lumpur takes 12 hours. The[re] are plenty of taxis and buses at the railway st[a]tion that will take you to the ferry terminal[.]

Right: close to 100,000 vehicles cross the Penang Bridge every day

y Road

here is no physical link between Langkawi
d the mainland. However, you can go by
ad on the North-South Highway up to
nang, Kuala Kedah or Kuala Perlis, and
ke a ferry from there *(see By Sea below
d Penang/By Road on page 83).* Kuala
rlis is the closest point to the island and
out an hour north of Kuala Kedah.

Many express buses go to Penang, Alor
tar (for Kuala Kedah) and Kangar (for
uala Perlis). At Alor Setar and Kangar, take
axi or another bus to the coastal towns to
tch the ferry. Recommended companies
e **Plusliner/Nice** (tel: 03-2072 0763;
ww.plusliner.com) and **Sri Maju Sarata/
neka Jasaramai** (tel: 03-2070 1279;
ww.srimaju.com).

Kuala Perlis to the Thai border takes just
) minutes by car; via the highway, it is six
urs from Kuala Lumpur and another four
om Johor Bahru and Singapore. If you are
iving, leave your car at the ferry terminal
r park for a fee. Have change available
r tolls (about RM55 from Kuala Lumpur
Kuala Perlis and Kuala Kedah) and note
here the petrol stations are (for an express-
ay map, look up www.plus.com.my).

y Sea

here are numerous ferry services to
angkawi from Penang, Kuala Kedah and
uala Perlis in Malaysia, and Satun in Thai-
nd. Ferries are modern, air-conditioned
d carry between 90 and 220 passengers
angkawi Ferry Services, www.langkawi
rry.com). The ferries from Kuala Kedah
d Kuala Perlis run every half hour from
m–7pm. The journey to Langkawi is 90
inutes from Kuala Perlis and two hours
om Kuala Kedah. The ferry from Penang
aves at 8.45am and 3.30pm and the jour-
y takes two hours. There are three ferry
rvices daily to Langkawi from Satun and
e journey is 45 minutes. The jetty terminal
Langkawi is in Kuah, where you can eas-
y get taxis to your hotel or rent a car. Hotels
pickups from here too.

Cruise ships also call on Penang and
angkawi from Singapore and Port Klang
ear Kuala Lumpur), and these go up to
nuket too. You can take a one-way trip.
ontact **Star Cruises** (tel: 03-309 2828).

TRAVEL ESSENTIALS

When to Visit

Both islands are fine to visit all year round,
with sunny tropical weather and daytime
temperatures reaching 33°C (91°F) and
night-time temperatures falling to 25°C (°F).
Humidity is above 80 percent. Because
Malaysia is in the tropical belt, rain is common, usually in the evening; Langkawi is
wet between July and October. Langkawi
also experiences a marked dry season from
December–February, which sees a change in
its vegetation.

Every seven years or so, Malaysia feels
the effects of El Nino in the form of haze,
most of it blown by the southwest monsoon
from forest fire areas in Indonesia. July,
before the rains begin, is when the haze
usually occurs. Although Malaysia is not in
an earthquake zone, a tsunami hit both
islands in December 2004. While there were
some deaths and millions of ringgit of
damage, both islands have completely recov-
ered. Check the Malaysian Meteorological
Service site for details and updates
(www.kjc.gov.my).

Holiday periods can be crowded, specifically the Malaysian and Singaporean school
holidays, the festival periods of Chinese New
Year, Hari Raya Puasa, Deepavali and
Christmas, and long weekends.

Visas & Passports

Visa requirements change, so before travelling, check with the relevant Malaysian
embassy/consulate or on the **Immigration**
website (www.imi.gov.my). Citizens of the
Commonwealth (except Bangladesh, India,
Pakistan, Sri Lanka and Nigeria), ASEAN
countries, the US, Switzerland, the Nether-
lands, San Marino and Liechtenstein do not
need a visa to visit. Some EU, South American, South African and Arab nationals do not
need a visa if the visit does not exceed three
months. **Passports** must have minimum six
months' validity at the time of entry. Tourist
visas may be extended at the Immigration
Department (tel: 03-8880 1000).

Customs

When you arrive in Malaysia, you must
declare all dutiable or prohibited goods. Note

that possession of drugs carries a mandatory death sentence. Because Langkawi is a duty-free zone, you need a minimum 48-hour stay to be exempted from duty when you leave. There are tax exemption limits on alcohol (not more than 1L), tobacco (225g or 200 cigarettes), portable electrical or battery-operated appliances for personal care and hygiene and gifts and souvenirs (not over RM400 in value; RM500 for Langkawi).

Clothing

Light and loose clothes work best in Malaysia's climate, so pack cottons and natural fibres. Sunglasses, mosquito repellent, sunblock, and umbrellas or raincoats are advisable. Shoes should be removed before entering temples and homes, so slip-ons are handy. Shorts and T-shirts are generally acceptable, including in shopping malls.

Electricity

Power supply is 220 or 240 volts at 50Hz cycle. Most outlets use three-pin, flat-pronged plugs and many hotels have 110-volt shaving sockets.

Time Differences

Malaysia is eight hours ahead of GMT. Sunrise is around 6.45am and sunset 7.20pm.

GETTING ACQUAINTED

Geography & Population

Penang island measures 285sq km (110sq miles) and is dominated by a granite hill backbone rising up to 833m (2,733ft). Penang Hill is marginally lower than that. About half the island is hilly, of which about 15 percent is over 300m (984ft) above sea level. The natural vegetation is mostly mixed dipterocarp forest, and only 17 percent remains gazetted as forest reserves. Agriculture and urban development make up the rest of the area.

The most densely populated state in Malaysia, Penang is home to 1.2 million people from a diverse mix of cultures and religions. Chinese make up the majority, while Malays and the Arab diaspora are a close second. There are also various groups from the Indian subcontinent, as well as Thais, Burmese and Eurasians.

Langkawi is located north of Penang o the Thai-Malaysian sea border. Comprehen sive research on its geology reveals it to b of great biological interest, with the olde rock providing a base for younger formation through various periods. The rocks domina the middle of the islands and are covered wi ancient rainforests, mainly mixed dipter carp forest, with features that are more com mon in Thailand than the Peninsula.

Once home to a small population c Malay and Thai fishermen, Langkawi no has a population of 60,000. The majority the newcomers are mainlanders.

Government & Economy

Penang and Kedah are among Malaysia's 1 states and three federal territories. Nine state including Kedah, have sultans but their rol is mostly ceremonial. The other states lik Penang, are ruled by Governors or Yan Di-pertua. The political system is a consti tutional monarchy with the King, or the Yan di-Pertuan Agong, elected every five year on a rotational basis by the nine sultans.

As a former British colony, Malaysia legal and economic systems owe the origins to Britain. There are two houses c parliament – the lower house or Dewa Rakyat, and the senate or Dewan Negar Some members of the senate are appointe by the Yang di-Pertuan Agong while othe are elected by the legislatures of individu states. General elections are held once ever five years and the current government is coalition of Barisan Nasional parties, wit Dato' Seri Abdullah Ahmad Badawi as th Prime Minister. State governments ar elected for the same period of office but the is no upper house.

Malaysia's economic policies emphasi 'balanced development' among the ethni groups within the framework of rapid grow with equity as its primary thrust. Malaysi has set itself the economic goal of reachin developed nation status by 2020, mo recently by developing Malaysia into knowledge-based society. Spurred by 8. percent growth in the 1990s, Malaysi became one of the top 20 largest tradin nations in the world. The US is Malaysia largest trading partner, followed by Singa pore, Northeast Asia, Japan and ASEAN.

After the 1997 Asian financial crisis, measures to strengthen the financial sector and economic fundamentals were implemented, including capital controls such as pegging the ringgit to the US dollar. From 2001–4, Malaysia maintained an average 3 percent per annum growth. The 2005 lifting of capital controls is expected to stimulate the economy and attract more investment.

Malaysia's main exports are manufactured products, particularly electrical and electronic products, with Penang producing a sizeable amount of this. Other exports are crude oil and palm oil, with Malaysia being one of the world's largest exporters of palm oil.

Religion

The official religion is Islam, but there is freedom of worship. Islam is practised predominantly by the Malays. In Penang, many Muslims are Indian. Most Chinese are Buddhists or Taoists, but a large number are Christians of various denominations. Most Indians are Hindus or Christians. There are some Sikhs and Bahai, while most indigenous people practise animism.

How Not To Offend

Shoes should be removed before entering a Malaysian home or place of worship. When in a mosque, visitors who are inappropriately dressed will be provided with a robe; women should avoid wearing short skirts or shorts, and cover their heads with a scarf.

Pointing with the forefinger, pointing your feet at a person or touching a person's head are all considered rude. Shaking hands is acceptable but not hugging or kissing someone's cheek. Some Muslim women, especially those who wear a headscarf, and some Muslim men prefer not to shake hands with members of the opposite sex. So a nod or smile will do. Avoid public displays of affection.

It is rude to address another person by their first name, especially if it's an older person. The polite forms of address are, for men, *encik* (Mr) or *pakcik* (Uncle) and for women, *puan* (Mrs) or *makcik* (Aunty).

MONEY MATTERS

Currency, Money Exchange & ATMs

The currency in Malaysia is the ringgit (RM), which consists of notes in 100, 50, 10, and 1 ringgit denominations and coins of 50, 20, 10, 5 and 1 sen. RM1 is equivalent to 100 sen. Malaysians often use the word 'dollar' when referring to the ringgit.

Money can be exchanged at banks (Mon–Fri 9.30am–4pm, Sat 9.30am–12.30pm) and licensed moneychangers. Some moneychangers offer better rates than the banks. Travellers' cheques are accepted at major hotels, shopping centres and restaurants, but banks give you the best rates. Major hotels also exchange money for major currencies, but the rates are usually very bad.

In **Penang**, banks are along Lebuh Pantai; licensed moneychangers on Lebuh Pantai, Lebuh Chulia and Jln Kapitan Kling in Georgetown, and in Batu Feringgi (daily 8.30am–6pm). In **Langkawi**, the banks are in Kuah, and moneychangers in Kuah and Pantai Cenang. Most banks have ATMs. These machines are also found in or near larger shopping malls, and you can use your credit card to withdraw cash from these.

Credit Cards

VISA and Mastercard are accepted in major outlets. American Express and Diners Club are accepted in some restaurants and hotels. For lost cards, call **Visa** (tel: 1-800-800 159), **Mastercard** (tel: 1-800-804 594), **American Express** (daily 8am–9pm; tel: 03-2050 0888), **Diners Club** (office hours: tel: 03-2161 1055, after office hours: tel: 03-2161 2862).

Left: licensed moneychangers are widely available

Taxes & Tipping

A 5 percent government tax and 10 percent service charge are levied in restaurants. You may leave a small tip in restaurants and hotels, and for your tour guide if you are happy with the service. No tipping is required at hawker stalls, fast food restaurants or when taking taxis.

GETTING AROUND

Penang

Taxis

Taxis are abundant, but do not use meters, so agree on the price before you move off. Check fares with your hotel. Taxis charge RM5–8 for short distances within the city, and RM25 to Batu Ferringhi (RM30 at night). Taxis can also be hired for RM25 per hour. Negotiate prices for an all-day or several-day hire. Taxi stands are plentiful, but you can just flag one down.

Buses

The main bus terminals are at KOMTAR and the jetty (Pengkalan Weld), and from here, you can get to just about anywhere on the island and even to Butterworth. Most buses use coin machines, so make sure you have enough small change. Fares charged are based on the distance travelled, and only minibuses charge a flat rate of 80 sen.

Trishaws

Trishaws are a unique way of sightseeing Georgetown. Saved by the tourist trade, this three-wheeled vehicle is usually powered by old men who look far too frail to ferry burly Europeans around. Trishaws used to be one of the most common means of transport on the Peninsula, but have now all but disappeared except in Penang and a few other places. Agree on the price before you hire a trishaw. Fares are RM5 per km; per-hour rates are RM30, but negotiate if you are hiring a trishaw for a longer period.

Car Rental

Driving is enjoyable outside of Georgetown. Driving is on the left-hand side of the road and road signs are in Bahasa Malaysia. Observe the speed limit. An international

driving licence is required, except for tourists from the US, EU, Australia, New Zealand, Japan and Singapore. Rentals start from RM180 a day. Some agencies are **Avis** (tel: 04-643 9633; www.avis.com.my); **Budget** (tel: 04-210 8211; www.budget.com.my); **Hertz** (tel: 04-263 5914; www.hertz.com); **National** (tel: 04-643 4205; www.national-car.com); and **Orix** (tel: 1-800-881 55; www.orix.com.my).

Some agencies also offer car-and-driver packages. Make sure your drivers are licensed limo drivers. Freelance limo drivers are also plentiful; ask for them at your hotel or call **Shirleen Ang** (tel: 019-447 6804) or **Bernard Hong** (tel: 017-478 9655).

Bicycles & Motorcycles

Bicycles (RM10 a day) and motorcycles (from RM30 per day) are inexpensive and fun ways of exploring the island. Check that your motorcycle comes with insurance; drivers need a valid driving licence. Hire shops run along the hotel stretch of Batu Ferringhi and in the city, particularly the backpacker areas of Lebuh Chulia and Love Lane.

Guided Tours

Check at your hotel reception/tour desk for guided tours, which are conducted using air-conditioned coaches. Prices start at RM18 for a half-day tour. Reputable companies include **Tour East**, **Mayflower** and **Destination DE**. You could also hire a tour guide including heritage guides and nature specialists, through the **Penang Tourist Guide**

Above: sightseeing Georgetown by trishaw

sociation (daily 10am–6pm; tel: 04-261
61). For heritage tours, contact the **Penang
eritage Trust** (Mon–Fri 9am–5pm, Sat
m–1pm; tel: 04-264 2631). Guide fees are
M20–25 per hour, not including transport.

angkawi
ar Rental
1e best and most enjoyable way to get
ound Langkawi is to drive. The roads are
od, wide and mostly well signposted, par-
ularly for tourist attractions. Note that road
gns are in Bahasa Malaysia and driving is
the left-hand side of the road. Langkawi
s excellent roads, but resist speeding, as
ads pass through villages where children
d livestock regularly meander across the
ad, and forest areas where wildlife hang
t on the tarmac. At night, difficult-to-spot
ffaloes have a habit of wandering across
d even sitting in the middle of roads.

An international driving licence is required
cept for tourists from the US, EU,
ustralia, New Zealand, Japan and
ngapore. Some car rental agencies have
fices at the airport, in town and in Pantai
enang. Car rentals start from RM40 a day,
cluding insurance, but can double in the
ak season. If you are not sure about driving,
any car owners double as guides; they will
pear as soon as you get off the ferry or air-
ane. Some agencies to contact are: **Kasina**
l: 04-955 5999; www.kasina.com.my),
ahamas (tel: 04-966 5981); **MBO Rental**
antai Cenang tel: 04-9551939).

icycles
ploring Langkawi by bicycle (RM12 a day)
motorcycle (from RM25 per day) can really
aximise the holiday resort feel. Cyclists
ould note that some parts of Langkawi are
ry hilly. Motorcyclists need a valid driv-
g licence and should check that the bike
re comes with insurance. You can hire these
hicles in Kuah or at any of the beaches.

axis
axis are plentiful and the main means of
ablic transport on the island, but only run
om 6am–midnight. They do not use meters
determine fares before you set off. Fares
e also listed at taxi stations. Flagging down
axi from the road is acceptable. Taxis seat

four to 12 and charge RM4 per passenger
from Kuah to Pantai Cenang if there is a
minimum of four passengers. A four-pas-
senger taxi can be rented for RM20 an hour.

HOURS & HOLIDAYS
Penang
Business Hours
Business days are from Monday to Friday
(9am–6pm) and half day on Saturday
(9am–1pm). Government departments and
some business establishments work five-day
weeks (Mon–Thur 8.30am–12.30pm, 1.30–
5.30pm; Fri 8.30am–12.45pm, 2.45–
4.45pm). Shopping malls open daily from
11am–9pm while retail outlets are usually
open from 9am–7pm.

Langkawi
Business Hours
Business days are from Saturday to Wednesday (9am–6pm) and half day on Thursday
(9am–1pm). Friday is a rest day. Government departments and some business establishments work five-day weeks (Sat–Wed
8.30am–12.30pm, 1.30–5.30pm; Thur
8.30am–12.45pm, 2.45–4.45pm). Shopping
malls and retail outlets are generally open
every day from 11am–10pm.

Public Holidays
1 January – New Year's Day (Penang)
6 January – Birthday of Sultan of Kedah
(Langkawi)
25 January – Thaipusam (Penang)
End January/early February – Chinese
New Year
early April – Birthday of Prophet
Muhammad
1 May – Labour Day
early May – Wesak Day
4 June – Birthday of the Yang di-Pertuan
Agong of Langkawi (Langkawi)
9 July – Birthday of Yang di-Pertuan of
Penang (Penang)
31 August – National Day
mid-October – Nurul Al-Quran (Penang)
early November – Deepavali
25 December – Christmas
Movable holidays: Hari Raya Puasa, Hari
Raya Haji, Awal Muharram

practical information

ACCOMMODATION

Hotels for every budget are available in Penang and Langkawi. Hotels, regardless of whether they are international chains or home-grown ventures, are star-rated from 1 to 5 according to modified international criteria such as size, facilities, number of staff and safety. For details, check out the **Malaysian Association of Hotels** website, www.hotels.org.my. Budget accommodation includes dormitories, homestays and rooms with shared amenities.

Hotels must quote net prices, and most include breakfast with the room. Actual rates are usually lower than published rates, and discounts can be negotiated for a longer stay. Ask about packages. Book in advance during Malaysian and Singaporean school holidays and public holidays, particularly long weekends. A guide to published rates for standard double rooms is as follows:

$ = below RM100
$$ = RM100–199
$$$ = RM200–399
$$$$ = RM400 and above

Penang

Tourists in Penang stay either in town for a cultural experience or at the beach for a resort holiday. Transport between town and the beach is not a problem, but traffic can be heavy during peak hours. In town, backpackers are catered to with pre-war buildings in Little India, Chulia Street and Love Lane, although some have insalubrious 'massage parlours' signages attached. Beach budget accommodation is found in Batu Ferringhi village in the form of homestays.

GEORGETOWN
E&O Hotel
10 Lebuh Farquhar
Tel: 04-263 0630
www.e-o-hotel.com
From its white colonial facade to the porters' uniforms, Penang's Grand Old Lady retains its 1885 charm. Its 101 suites have views of the sea or of the city, spacious bathrooms, as well as modern amenities such as wireless access and luxurious personalised service. Sundowners at the Farquhar Bar will certainly evoke Somerset Maugham and

Rudyard Kipling, after whom the hotel suites are named. **$$$$**

Cheong Fatt Tze Mansion
14 Leith Street
Tel: 04-262 0006
www.cheongfatttzemansion.com
This 19th-century landmark mansion famed for its architecture and *feng shui* offers an unforgettable place to stay. Each of the 16 unique rooms with en-suite bathroom contains period furniture and antiques. A personal valet service completes the experience at this boutique hotel. **$$$**

Shangri-la Hotel
Magazine Road
Tel: 04-262 2622
www.shangri-la.com/penang/shangri-la/e
Situated next to KOMTAR as well as the shopping and heritage areas, this 440-room hotel has the facilities you would expect to find in five-star accommodation. It has a good fitness centre, which includes a gynasium, spa and swimming pools. Its Shang Palace restaurant is expensive, but provides a beautiful dining experience. Guests can also use facilities at Golden Sands Resort, the sister hotel at the beach. **$$$**

Sheraton Penang
3 Jalan Larut
Tel: 04-226 7888
www.sheraton.com/penang
Located midway between the city centre and Gurney Drive, each of the 237 rooms in the

Above: courtyard area at the Cathay Hotel

e-star hotel has a nice view and a balcony. he hotel has a reputation for good service. tracting mainly a business clientele, it has cilities such as a direct fax line and broad- nd Internet. **$$$**

ty Bayview Hotel
A Lebuh Farquhar
l: 04-263 3161, 1-800-888 854
vw.bayviewintl.com
his value-for-money hotel is within walk- g distance to shopping, historical land- arks, pubs and restaurants. Upper floors ve great views of the bay, and for a 360° ew, visit the Revolving Restaurant. There a free shuttle service to the hotel's sister sort on the beach. **$$**

titel Penang Hotel
Penang Road
l: 04-370 1188, 1-800-383 388 (toll-free)
vw.cititelhotel.com
a great location on Penang Road with taxi d trishaw stations, and entertainment out- ts on its doorstep, this four-star business tel is popular with tourists. Although the oms are not large, they are clean and afford vely views from the top storeys. **$$**

athay Hotel
Leith Street
l: 04-262 6271
uilt in 1902, this atmospheric old wooden

colonial villa, which has been the location set for two movies, is a popular budget hotel, with large clean rooms and decent, if worn, furnishings. A former millionaire's mansion, it has 37 rooms, with the top range getting you a fairly colossal space complete with hot water and air-conditioning. There are also fan-only rooms. **$**

Oasis Hotel
23 Lorong Cinta (Love Lane)
Tel: 04-261 6778
A century-old former private residence, this place has a good reputation among back- packers. A welcoming orange archway opens into a restful sanctuary where an unas- suming bungalow is surrounded by shady trees. Cooking facilities and self-service laundry are available. Travel arrangements can also be made here. **$**

GURNEY DRIVE
Evergreen Laurel
53 Persiaran Gurney
Tel: 04-226 9988
www.evergreen-hotels.com
Located right on Gurney Drive and within walking distance to the food areas, this Taiwanese-owned five-star hotel has suites directly facing the bay – and therefore great oceanfront views. The hotel has a bright and cheerful atmosphere, and it is also handi- cap accessible. It also has a nice swimming

bove: the atmospheric E&O Hotel

pool, a gymnasium, jacuzzi, great breakfasts and a fun lounge. $$$

The Gurney
18 Persiaran Gurney
Tel: 04-370 7000
www.gurney-hotel.com.my
Located at the end of Gurney Drive, its selling point is its very large suites that have almost-ceiling-to-floor views of Gurney Drive; the best views are from the rooms closest to the sea. The equally spacious bathrooms are equipped with jacuzzi bathtubs. The hotel's Recreational Park is great for kids, and there is also a popular club, a few cafés and some shops. $$$

BATU FERRINGHI
Golden Sands Resort
Batu Ferringgi Beach
Tel: 04-881 1911
www.shangri-la.com
Part of the Shangri-la chain, this 395-room family-friendly resort has good facilities, including a lovely poolside bar and a famous Mediterranean restaurant. Get a room overlooking the lagoon-style swimming pools. Guests also have signing privileges at its sister hotel in the city and towards the end of 2006 (when it reopens after a complete makeover) at the neighbouring Rasa Sayang luxury resort. $$$$

Grand Plaza Parkroyal
Batu Ferringhi Beach
Tel: 04-881 1133
www.grandplaza.penang.parkroyalhotels.com
The rather austere exterior belies the relaxed resort feel inside. Newly renovated, it has wonderful free-form swimming pools, a nice beachside sunset bar and well-tended gardens. The airy lobby is home to a comfortable lounge/bar. There is also a club for children. $$$

Lone Pine Resort
97 Batu Ferringhi
Tel: 04-881 1511/1512
www.lonepinehotel.com
With only 50 rooms, Ferringhi's first hotel has a laid-back, 1970s feel, complete with marquees and inviting hammocks on the extensive beachfront lawn. Managed by the

E&O Hotel, the seafront ground-level room with verandas are nicest; other rooms ha private courtyards. $$$

Ferringhi Beach Hotel
Jalan Low Yat, off Batu Ferringhi Road
Tel: 04-890 5999, 1800-88 8299 (toll-fre
www.ferringhi.com.my
For a no-frills hotel in a quiet location, lo no further. Although there is slightly dat feel to it and the hotel is located across fro the beach, the rooms are a good size a clean. Overall, it offers a nice family env ronment. In addition, meals, including roo service, are reasonably priced. It costs on RM1 to get to the main Batu Ferringhi stret by bus. $$

Ali's Guest House & Restaurant
53 & 54B Batu Ferringhi
Tel: 04-8811 1316
e-mail: alisguesthouse_pg@yahoo.com
This established backpacker's guesthouse the Batu Ferringhi village has been upgrade to include rooms with attached bathroom air-conditioning and hot showers. A few fa cooled rooms with common baths are als available. The restaurant-and-pub is sit ated in a lovely garden. $

Shalini's Guest House
56 Batu Ferringhi
Tel: 04-881 1859
e-mail: ahlooi@pc.jaring.my
This clean, friendly homestay run by a Ch nese-Indian couple and their family offe

a choice of rooms with attached baths and air-conditioning, or common baths and fans. Breakfast is included only during the peak tourist season. $

Langkawi

Most of the accommodation here is of the first-class beach resort variety. Pantai Cenang/Pantai Tengah have a variety of hotels, including lower budget accommodation, while the northern, more isolated beaches have cornered the luxury market. Anywhere a hotel is close to a rainforest, watch out for monkeys, which can be a nuisance. Accommodation is often booked out in December during the Lima Exhibition and over the Christmas/New Year period.

KUAH

Sheraton Perdana Resort
Jalan Pantai Dato Syed Omar
Tel: 04-966 2020
www.sheraton.com/perdana
This 200-room five-star hotel close to Kuah has a good range of facilities, including three swimming pools and easy access to golf and diving. Most rooms have a balcony opening up to ocean views. There is no beach to speak of, but paths and steps take you through mature gardens. It has a sister resort on the beach. $$$

NORTHERN BEACHES

The Andaman
Jalan Teluk Datai
Tel: 04-959 1088
www.theandaman.com
Set in rainforest and overlooking the beautiful white beach and blue waters of Teluk Datai, this family-friendly hotel has 188 Malay-style rooms and suites. Service is excellent, even for children, and facilities are superb. Enjoy tasty curries at the Gulai House and chill out with cocktails and live entertainment at the Lobby Lounge. $$$$

The Datai
Jalan Teluk Datai
Tel: 04-959 2500
www.thedatai.com
This sophisticated sister hotel to the Andaman on Teluk Datai is also set spectacularly in the rainforest, with wood featuring extensively in its public spaces and its widely spaced out rooms, which comprise 54 deluxe rooms, 40 villas and 18 suites. Quiet and geared towards couples, it boasts restaurants with good food and an excellent wine list, and a must-try spa. $$$$

Four Seasons
Jalan Tanjung Rhu
Tel: 04-950 8812
www.fourseasons.com/langkawi
Space is what this luxurious new Islamic/ Spanish-style resort offers in its large, well-appointed rooms, as well as the attention to privacy. Set against beautiful virgin rainforest and limestone hills and with mangroves on its doorstep, the nature tours are worth taking. $$$$

PANTAI CENANG/PANTAI TENGAH

Bon Ton Restaurant and Resort
Pantai Cenang
Tel: 04-955 6787
www.bontonresort.com.my
What began as a restaurant has become a rustic boutique hotel comprising seven century-old Malay houses painstakingly sourced and reassembled here. The homely chalets are equipped with modern bathrooms and mosquito arsenal, and you get a healthy breakfast in your fridge when you wake up. A variety of cats are permanent guests. Efficient staff can arrange tours and cruises. Located five minutes from the main beach of Pantai Cenang. $$$

Above: pristine forest is the setting for The Datai

Pelangi Beach and Spa Resort
Pantai Cenang
Tel: 04-952 8888
www.pelangibeachresort.com
Comprising 350 spacious single and double-storey wooden Malay *kampung* or village-style houses, this five-star resort spreads over lovely gardens and a beachfront. Its kids' club has extensive activities from 9am–9pm, while its spa's signature treatments draw on Malay/Indonesian and Thai traditions. **$$$$**

Beach Garden Resort Bistro and Beergarden
Pantai Cenang
Tel: 04-955 1363
www.beachgardenresort.com
An intimate, German-run resort, its 12 rooms are sparse and have no telephone or TV. The swimming pool is also tiny, but the landscaping of lush greenery is lovely and kilometres of beautiful beach are right on the resort's doorstep. The excellent beachside bistro serves great margaritas and pizza, and the breakfasts are sumptuous. **$$**

Langkawi Village Resort
Jalan Teluk Baru, Pantai Tengah
Tel: 04-955 1511
www.langkawi-villageresort.com
This three-star resort sits right on a sublime coconut tree-fringed beach with a view of islands. Spacious chalets with charming outdoor bathrooms sit in rows on the beach while double-storey rooms are behind. Under a new management, the resort is gradually being converted into a four-star boutique hotel and spa. **$$**

Malibest Resort
Pantai Cenang
Tel: 04-955 8222
e-mail: malibestlgk@yahoo.com
Five treetop chalets are the star attraction of this newly renovated resort, which is located close to eateries and shops. Catering to medium- and low-budget tourists, it also has 58 wooden chalets, two 20-person dormitories and even more accommodation across the road. Some rooms have air-conditioning, hot water and a fridge. Reception is open from 7am–11pm. **$$**

AB Motel
Pantai Cenang
Tel: 04-955 1300
e-mail: abmotel@hotmail.com
An established backpacker hotel, this 50 room concern has been recently upgraded and now comprises all-brick air-conditioned chalets. The chalets are clean and there are some lovely beachside units. An attached restaurant serves Malay food. Facilities include Internet access, bicycle and motor bike hire as well as tours. Reception is open from 7am–midnight. **$**

HEALTH & EMERGENCIES

Hygiene & General Health
It is advisable to drink only boiled and bottled water, or bottled and canned drinks. Mineral and bottled water is widely available. Avoid ice cubes at street-side stalls and small coffeeshops, as they are usually made from unboiled tap water. To be on the safe side, refrain from eating cut fruit in stalls. Otherwise, the food served in restaurants and hawker centres is generally safe.

Public toilets can be dirty, and many still only have squat toilets. Toilets in hotels tend be the best option. Pharmacies, which can easily be found in most shopping centres are well stocked and have registered phar

Left: the Bon Ton Restaurant and Resort is a cosy boutique hotel

macists. Controlled drugs are sold only by prescription, so pack any medicine you need.

Crime

The emergency number for police is 999, for an ambulance is 911, and for fire is 994.

Penang

Pharmacies

Apex Pharmacy, Jalan Burma, tel: 04-228 5520

George Town Pharmacy, Lebuh Beach, tel: 04-261 0306

Guardian Pharmacy, Plaza Gurney, tel: 04-226 1649 (also at KOMTAR, Prangin Mall, Kompleks Bukit Jambul, Penang Plaza, Tanjung Bungah, Island Plaza)

Hovid Pharmacy, Bandar Baru, Ayer Itam, tel: 04-829 0799

YW Cheah Farmasi, Jalan Burmah, tel: 04-226 5819

Medical/Dental Services

Twenty-four-hour medical clinics and dental clinics are plentiful in Georgetown and Batu Ferringhi.

Adventist Hospital, Jalan Burma, Georgetown, tel: 04-226 1133

General Hospital, Jalan Utama, Georgetown, tel: 04-229 3333

Hospital Lam Wah Ee, Jalan Tan Sri Teh Ewe Lim, Georgetown, tel: 04-657 1888

Loh Guan Lye Specialists Centre, Logan Road, Georgetown, tel: 04-228 8501

Klinik Ferringhi, Batu Ferringhi (opposite Yahong Art Gallery), tel: 04-881 1491

Langkawi

Pharmacies

Joe's Pharmacy, Kuah, tel: 04-966 0180

Medical & Dental Services

There are no 24-hour clinics in Langkawi, but its international hospital has some of the best facilities and doctors in the world as Langkawi also promotes 'health tourism'.

Langkawi International Hospital, Kuah, tel: 04-966 3333

Klinik Keluarga (Family Clinic), Jalan Panak Mayah 5 (in front of Saga Shopping Centre) Kuah, tel: 04-966 9048

Padang Matsirat Government Clinic, Jalan Padang Matsirat, tel: 04-955 1355

Pusat Perubatan Langkawi, Jalan Kisap, Kuah, tel: 04-966 2182

Klinik Pergigian Langkawi (Dental Clinic), Jalan Penarak, Kuah, tel: 04-966 7716

Klinik Pergigian Chew (Dental Clinic), Langkawi Mall, Kuah, tel: 04-966 0661

COMMUNICATIONS & NEWS

Post

Post offices here handle all the usual mail needs, including courier services. In **Penang**, the General Post Office is in Lebuh Downing, Georgetown (Mon–Fri 9am–5pm). You can also make international calls 24 hours a day from the Telekom office here. There is also a post office in Batu Ferringhi, opposite Grand Plaza Parkroyal. In **Langkawi**, the General Post Office is in Kompleks Lada, Kuah (Sat–Thur 8am–4.30pm). There is a post office in Padang Matsirat. Most big hotels can mail letters for guests.

Telephones & Internet

All hotels except for the most basic have IDD (international direct dial) facilities in the guestrooms. To call abroad, dial the international access code, 00, followed by the country code and the phone number. Hotels can also handle faxes. Hotels with a 4-star and above rating have business centres with computers and the Internet. Broadband wireless Internet is often available for a fee in business centres and in the guestrooms at luxury hotels.

Telephone calls from public telephone booths cost a flat rate of 10 sen. For international calls, buy a prepaid phone card, available in RM5, RM10, RM20, RM50 and RM100 denominations. There are many other IDD phone cards available that offer discounted rates for international calls. Buy these at a mobile phone shops or at grocery stores. For directory assistance, dial 103, and international assisted service, 101.

If your mobile phone operates on the GSM network, you can bring it to Malaysia and buy a local prepaid SIM card, either DIGI (at RM18 for 30 days that includes a call value of RM10) or Hotlink (at RM20 for

60-day Active Period inclusive of RM10 air-time and rebate).

Internet cafés are plentiful, particularly around the backpacker areas, such as Jalan Chulia and Batu Ferringhi in Penang and Pantai Cenang in Langkawi. Note that some Internet cafés, particularly those with tinted glass windows, are actually gaming stations, and do not offer facilities for checking e-mail. Rates are about RM5 an hour. Many coffeehouse chains also have free broadband wireless Internet for customers.

Media

There are several English-language dailies, including *The Star*, *The New Straits Times* and *Malay Mail*. The first two offer comprehensive coverage of local and international news. Business coverage is provided weekly by *The Edge*. You can also buy *The Asian Wall Street Journal*, *The International Herald Tribune* and *USA Today* as well as leading international periodicals and magazines at bookshops and hotel newsstands.

Cable TV including CNN, CNBC and HBO is available in most hotels. Free-to-air local TV stations are run by state-owned RTM and private enterprises, the most popular being TV3 and NTV7. All stations air local and international news reports, often in English, as well as mainstream American sitcoms and movies and religious Islamic programmes.

FM radio has a range of English-language broadcasts, and these all feature mainly international chart toppers. English-language news is broadcast hourly. Other stations play everything from canto-pop to Bollywood film hits and Malay rock tunes.

LANGUAGE

Even though Bahasa Malaysia is the national language, Malaysians are generally multilingual, with most able to speak English or at least understand it.

Bahasa Malaysia is polysyllabic, with variations in syllables to convey changes in meaning, and words are pronounced as they are spelt. In general the pronunciation is the same as in English, with some exceptions: 'a' is pronounced 'ar' as in tar; 'e' has an 'er' sound as in reserve; 'c' is pronounced 'ch' as in chair and the 'g' is always hard as in gun; 'sy' is pronounced 'sh'.

Here is a small vocabulary list to get you on your way:

Numbers

1	*Satu*
2	*Dua*
3	*Tiga*
4	*Empat*
5	*Lima*
6	*Enam*
7	*Tujuh*
8	*Lapan*
9	*Sembilan*
10	*Sepuluh*
11	*Sebelas*
12	*Dua belas*
20	*Dua puluh*
21	*Dua puluh satu*
100	*Seratus*
1,000	*Seribu*

Greetings & Pleasantries

How do you do?	*Apa khabar?*
Good morning	*Selamat pagi*
Good afternoon	*Selamat petang*
Good night	*Selamat malam*
Goodbye	*Selamat tinggal*
Bon voyage	*Selamat jalan*
Fine/good	*Baik*
Thank you	*Terima kasih*

Above: *The Star*, the largest English language newspaper, was born in Penang

practical information

Please	Tolong/sila
Excuse me	Maafkan saya
I am sorry	Saya minta maaf
You're welcome	Sama-sama
What is your name?	Siapa nama anda?
My name is…	Nama saya…
Please be careful	Berhati-hati
Yes	Ya
No	Tidak

Prounouns

I	Saya
You	Anda/awak
He/she	Dia
We	Kami
They	Mereka

Forms of Address

Mr	Encik
Mrs	Puan
Miss	Cik

Direction & Driving

Where	Di mana
Right	Kanan
Left	Kiri
Turn	Belok
Go	Pergi
Stop	Berhenti
Follow	Ikut
Near	Dekat
Far	Jauh
Inside	Dalam
Outside	Luar
Front	Hadapan/Depan
Behind	Belakang
Here	Sini
There	Sana
Road	Jalan
Lane	Lorong
Street	Lebuh
Bridge	Jambatan
Junction	Simpang
Danger	Awas/Merbahaya
One-way street	Jalan Sehala
North	Utara
South	Selatan
East	Timur
West	Barat

Useful Phrases

How much?	Berapa harganya?
Can you help?	Bolehkah cik tolong?

Where is this place?	Di mana tempat ini?
How far?	Berapa jauh?
I want to go to…	Saya hendak pergi ke…
Stop here	Tolong berhenti di sini
Expensive	Mahal
Lower the price	Kurangkan harganya
Too big	Besar sangat
Too small	Kecil sangat
Any other colour?	Ada warna lain?

Other Handy Words

Drink	Minum (verb), Minimum (noun)
Eat	Makan (verb), Makanan (noun)
When?	Bila?
Hot (spicy)	Pedas
Hot (heat)	Panas
Cold	Sejuk
Sweet	Manis
Sour	Masam
Delicious	Sedap
Clean	Bersih
Dirty	Kotor
Beautiful	Cantik
Open	Buka
Close	Tutup
Never	Tidak pernah
Often	Selalu
Sometimes	Kadang-kadang

USEFUL INFORMATION

Handicap Accessibility

Basic handicap-accessible facilities like extra-wide parking bays and toilets can be found in major hotels, malls, international fast food chains and some government buildings. In general, though, neither island is very disabled-friendly.

Children

Travelling in Penang and Langkawi with children is safe, but these places are not necessarily baby-friendly as there are inadequate facilities for breastfeeding, nappy changing and strollers. Hotels with a rating of four stars and above have kids' clubs, with activities and minders for children all day long. Some malls have play areas and fast-food chains to keep children happy. In Langkawi, **Natural History Expeditions** (tel: 04-959 4772; www.malaysia-wildlife. com) has excellent conservation programmes designed for 7- to 14-year-olds.

Maps

Complimentary tourist maps are available at the Airport, Tourist Information Centres and major hotels. See Useful Addresses, p.100, for Tourist Information Centre locations.

Penang
Bookshops

United Books, Jalan Penang
Popular Books, 2nd floor, KOMTAR; 5th–6th Floor, Onestop Midlands
Times The Bookshop, 1st Floor, Penang Plaza; 126, Burmah Road; Yaohan, Level 4, KOMTAR
MPH, Gurney Tower; Gurney Plaza
Kinokuniya Bookstore, Gama Supermarket & Departmental Store, 3rd Floor, Jalan Dato Keramat

There are a few **second-hand bookshops** on Lebuh Chulia.

SPORTS

Penang
Archery

Bull Eyes Archery, Prangin Mall, tel: 04-262 5262

Golf

The **Penang Turf Club Golf** (tel: 04-226 6701) is an 18-hole course near the Turf Club. It has a pro shop, driving range and restaurant. Green fees start at RM84 on weekdays. The **Bukit Jambul Country Club** (tel: 04-644 2255) is a beautiful 18-hole course next to the Equatorial Hotel in Bayan Lepas, with excellent facilities including restaurants, driving range, putting green, chipping and bunker practice area, pro shop, resident professional, changing rooms with sauna, function rooms and swimming pool. Green fees start at RM100 on weekdays.

Jungle Trekking/Nature Trips

Penang has numerous trails in all sorts of terrain, from beach to rainforest. The most comprehensive trekking guidebook is *Natu Trails of Penang Island* published by th Malaysian Nature Society. While the mo adventurous might wish to venture out o their own, it is safer and more informative have a trail guide. Contact **Forest Explore** at www.forestexplorers.com. Most **beac hotels** offer simple early morning guide treks. Picnics are usually provided.

Bird Watching

There are over 200 species of birds in Penan more than half of which are found in th forest. For tours, contact **Forest Explorer** (see above) or Dr Chan Lai Keng of th **Malaysian Bird Watching Society** (tel: 0 657 7888).

Hashing

The **Hash House Harriers** was actual started in the 1930s in Kuala Lumpur b some British expats. The tradition of a ru followed by some beer at the pub continue today. Check out trails and hash schedules www.malaysiahash.com.

Other Sports

In December, **Penang International Spor Arena** (PISA) on Jalan Tun Dr Awang (te 04-646 2564) is the venue for the state's ol est sports event. The community **Starwal** attracts 10,000 participants. This is also th venue for the **Malaysian Dancesport cham pionships**. There is also the internation **Penang Bridge Run**, which is held in th

Above: the Brown-winged Kingfisher is unique to Langkawi

practical information

iddle of the year. There are full, half and uarter marathon events.

angkawi

Golf

angkawi's 18-hole golf courses are scenic, ell designed and have good facilities. The angkawi Golf Club (tel: 04-966 6187) on alan Bukit Malut on the outskirts of Kuah a beachfront, full buggy and caddy course. reen fees are RM80. The **Gunung Raya Golf Resort** (tel: 04-966 8148) was designed y renowned American architect Max Vexler. Green fees are RM200. In the north the beautiful championship course of the **Golf Club Datai Bay** (tel: 04-959 2620). Green fees are RM180.

ungle Trekking & Nature Trips

Numerous trails and rivers wind through angkawi's age-old rainforest. Langkawi as some excellent and professional nature uides who have a range of packages or can ailor-make trips for different fitness levels, whether trekking, kayaking or boating. Con-act **Natural History Expeditions** (tel: 04-59 4772; www.malaysia-wildlife.com) or angkawi Canopy Adventures (tel: 012-84 8744; e-mail: juergzim@yahoo.com). rips range from RM100 to RM250.

Airtrekking

his is a unique and adrenalin-pumping way o experience the rainforest. Run by angkawi Canopy Adventures (tel: 012-84 8744; e-mail: juergzim@yahoo.com), it onsists of a series of three flying-fox rope ourses over the rainforest canopy as well as bseiling. The minimum age is 12 and prices tart at RM220.

Bird Watching

Approximately 220 species of birds have een recorded in the Langkawi archipelago. Among them, the Brown-winged Kingfisher, he Mountain Hawk-Eagle and Eurasian Golden Oriole are unique to the island. The est places for bird watching are at Gunung Raya, the paddy fields, and the Kilim and Kisap mangroves.

For organised tours, get in touch with **Natural History Expeditions** (tel: 04-959 772; www.malaysia-wildlife.com).

Sailing

With numerous rocky islands, secluded beaches and charming coves to explore, Langkawi offers pure sailing pleasure. A range of sailing options is available, whether full-day, half-day or sunset cruises on skippered yachts or bareboat charters. Book a couple of days beforehand during the low season (June–September); otherwise, give the company a week's notice.

Sunsail at the Royal Langkawi Yacht Club (daily 8.30am–5.30pm; tel: 04-966 5869; www.sunsail.com) have 23 yachts servicing Langkawi and Phuket. Depending on the size of the boat, day charter is RM300 per person with a minimum of four passengers, including lunch, drinks and a skipper. They even run sailing courses.

Bon Ton Restaurant and Resort (tel: 04-955 6787; www.bontonresort.com.my) offers wine and/or dine cruises as well as day charters on its 1940s vintage timber motor yacht. The 26-seater is berthed at Telaga Harbour and rates start at RM220.

Scuba Diving
Pulau Payar and **Ko Adang** in south Thailand has excellent diving and snorkelling. **East Marine** at the Royal Langkawi Yacht Club (tel: 04-966 3966; www.eastmarine.com.my) offers dive tours, dive instruction and Discover Scuba packages.

USEFUL ADDRESSES

Penang
TOURIST OFFICES
Tourist Information Centre
Bayan Lepas International Airport
Tel: 04-643 0501 (9am–5pm)
10 Jalan Tun Syed Sheh Barakbah
Tel: 04-262 0066 (9am–5pm)
www.tourismpenang.gov.my

Penang Tourist Centre
Pesara King Edward
Tel: 04-216 633 (Mon–Fri 8.30am–1pm, 2–4.30pm, Sat 8.30am–1pm)

Langkawi
TOURIST OFFICES
Tourist Information Centre
Jalan Persiaran Putra, Kuah
Tel: 04-966 7789 (9am–5pm)

FURTHER READING

There is far more written about Penang than Langkawi, although more literature for the tourist market is coming out on the latter. Here is a random reading list:

The Encyclopedia of Malaysia. An expanding collection of Malaysiana with lovely illustrations, covering such topics as plants, architecture, politics, economics, and early history (Archipelago Press).

Geoforest Parks: Hanging Gardens of Langkawi, by S.L.Wong. A beautiful photographic tribute to the geological wonders of Langkawi. (Forestry Department Peninsular Malaysia & Lestari UKM, 2005).

Harmony Silk Factory, by Tash Aw. A gripping tale of 1940s Malaya told from three perspectives in a 'mercurial debut' by this UK-based Malaysian author. (Fourth Estate, 2005).

The Malayan Trilogy, by Anthon Burgess. Satirical lyrical slapstick of th waning days of the British Empire (1964)

Nonya Flavours: A Complete Guide t Penang Straits Chinese Cuisine, edited b Julie Wong. A lovely collection of 150 illus trated recipes of famous Penang Nonya cui sine (Star Publications, 2003).

Paradoxes of Mahathirism: An Intellec tual Biography of Mahathir Mohamad b Khoo Boo Teik. A carefully researched stud on the former Prime Minister's ideas o nationalism, capitalism and Islam, amon other topics (1995).

Penang Sketchbook by Chin Kon Yit. A elegant 150-watercolour overview of th city's history, with architectural/historica commentaries (Archipelago Press, 2002).

Selected Nature Trails of Penang Islan by Ang Sek Chuan. Maps, trail description and information on the island's natural his tory (Malaysian Nature Society Penan Branch, Penang: 1999).

Streets of Georgetown Penang by Kho Su Nin. An excellent street-by-street guid to the historical landmarks of Penang, b Penang's top heritage conservationist (1993)

WEBSITES

The Official Website of Tourism Penang www.tourismpenang.gov.my. This site by th Penang Tourism Action Council is an excel lent resource for tourist related informatio including articles, activities and images.

The Penang Story. www.penangstory.net An account of the proceedings from the con ference that paved the way for Georgetown World Heritage list application.

Forest Explorers. www.forestexplorers com. This is an excellent site that cover nature and nature trails in Penang.

Best of Langkawi. www.best-of-langkawi com. Comprehensive resource of touris activities in Langkawi including articles b readers and detailed listings.

Kakiseni. www.kakiseni.com. An e-zin featuring contemporary Malaysian arts, wit quirky writing and spirited discourse.

Aliran. www.aliran.com. Alternativ news and information on Malaysia run b the country's foremost human rights grou

ACKNOWLEDGEMENTS

Front Cover	**Imagery and Imagination/Alamy**
Photography	**John Ishii/APA** and
43	**Chng Eu Lee**
80	**Jonathan Koh/APA**
14	**Private Archives**
15	**Jati/HBL**
40, 96	**SL Wong**
Cartography	**Verlag Wolfgang Kunth GmbH & Co. KG**
Cover Design	**Klaus Geisler**
Production	**Caroline Low**

© APA Publications GmbH & Co. Verlag KG Singapore Branch, Singapore

practical information

INDEX